# IRAQ
# AND
# BACK

Philip Woodhall

Printed in Victoria, BC, Canada

Note for Librarians: a cataloguing record for this book that includes Dewey Decimal Classification and US Library of Congress numbers is available from the Library and Archives of Canada. The complete cataloguing record can be obtained from their online database at:
www.collectionscanada.ca/amicus/index-e.html
ISBN 1-4120-4543-6

# TRAFFORD

This book was published on-demand in cooperation with Trafford Publishing. On-demand publishing is a unique process and service of making a book available for retail sale to the public taking advantage of on-demand manufacturing and Internet marketing. On-demand publishing includes promotions, retail sales, manufacturing, order fulfilment, accounting and collecting royalties on behalf of the author.

Offices in Canada, USA, UK, Ireland, and Spain
book sales for North America and international:
Trafford Publishing, 6E–2333 Government St.
Victoria, BC V8T 4P4 CANADA
phone 250 383 6864    toll-free 1 888 232 4444
fax 250 383 6804    email to orders@trafford.com

book sales in Europe:
Trafford Publishing (UK) Ltd., Enterprise House, Wistaston Road Business Centre
Crewe, Cheshire CW2 7RP UNITED KINGDOM
phone 01270 251 396    local rate 0845 230 9601
facsimile 01270 254 983    orders.uk@trafford.com

order online at:
www.trafford.com/robots/04-2351.html

10        9        8        7        6        5        4        3

# AUTHORS NOTE

**W**ho am I to write a book about Iraq?

Well to be perfectly honest, I am nobody, I'm certainly no political expert who can view the balance of a government's fragile position and give a strategic military viewpoint. I am definitely no NATO potato who can tell you what type of tank it was just by looking at the track prints in the sand through a pair of binoculars from 400 metres,

I'm just a regular man with a normal family life. A life filled with everything from the boredom and stress at work selling forklift trucks to the mundane Dads job of providing a taxi service to my three kids. I get grief from my wife when I forget to put my dirty washing in the basket and when it comes to the Dads race at the kids school sports day, I'm the first on the track armed only with a pair of trainers that I wear for cutting the grass and the pressure of my children's credibility resting firmly on my shoulders. I risk life and limb to cross the country, arriving in the nick of time to sit on a small plastic chair to see my child wearing a grey blanket and a cardboard mask playing the important role of a donkey in the Christmas nativity play. I find myself watching a film at home and mindlessly walking into the kitchen staring into the fridge with a blank gaze, knowing that there is nothing to eat because I did exactly the same thing during the last advert break and there was nothing then either, but here I am yet again, not knowing how I got here and still not finding anything to eat.

---

In short, I'm just like every other family man in the UK, being in that small minority of men who actually laughs *with* Homer Simpson not *at* him because we empathise with all that he has to deal with seeing ourselves with the same pressures of life.

So to find myself in the surreal world of leaving my family and going to a war zone for the first time, when I'm in the autumn of my thirty something years and having never spent longer than two weeks away from home before, was an experience that I felt I had to share with others, so they could try to understand how different life can become from the norm. And all of this, because I once saw an advert for the Territorial Army on the television...

# IRAQ AND BACK

Dedicated to

my wife Kerry

and my three children

Ashleigh, Alex and Georgia.

Also to my Mum, Joyce and

Dad, Brian for their

loving support.

———————

PHILIP WOODHALL

# PREFACE

**W**hatever we might think of the rights and wrongs of the operational demands of the conflict in Iraq, there are human responses which serving officers and soldiers cannot become involved in. We are both civilians and soldiers and we have a duty to do as ordered. That does not mean that we cannot feel that there are certain rights and wrongs, which are an issue for all of us. We have arrived in Iraq not to kill Iraqi's, but to clear the country of those Iraqis who would wage war on their own people and upon those who have been sent into Iraq to free the Iraqi people from a tyrannical rule. We all hear stories in the media of what Saddam Hussein did; we even see the videos of the worst crimes committed against innocent people over many years. For us to become this acclimatised to what has been happening in the world is a worry. For my children to grow up without the sight of such horrors will be a duty I will gladly undertake. There are concerns, there are worries, but they are the concerns of governments and the issues for the people who should have a voice to be heard. For us, soldiers in Iraq, it is our duty to uphold the best traditions of democracy we know everyone is entitled to, and yet proud to be a part of arguably the finest Army in the world just doing its job.

PHILIP WOODHALL

# THE DAY HAS ARRIVED

## 24th May 2003

The letter hit the doormat with a thud as I had been told it would, it was a warm Saturday morning late May 2003. There was no doubt about it, it was the one, a large A4 sized plain brown envelope with a Portsmouth postmark, and the day had come. I had known for a few days that it could arrive at any time, but that still doesn't make it any easier when it finally arrives. I slowly thumbed it open and gently removed the countless papers from within, finally revealing the letterhead addressed to me reading "COMPULSORY MOBILISATION". I now had three weeks to get my life in order, inform my employer and ready to present myself, bags packed for mobilisation, reporting to the

---

RTMC (Reservists Training and Mobilisation Centre) in Chilwell Nottingham, England at 1200hrs 16th June, 2003.

I could be going to Iraq.

The war had recently been declared over, but Saddam was still out there somewhere and at thirty-eight years old, a family man with three young children and a responsible career, I had no desires to rush out to look for him. I had a few friends from my Territorial Army unit in Nottingham that had already been called up in February and were out there already, starting off in Kuwait and pushing north into Iraq as the war developed. I was both surprised and very relieved when I didn't get the call up in February, but like most other people in the UK, I thought it was all over. How wrong I was!

I had never set out to join the Army when I left school but had always harboured a few regrets and dreams that maybe I should have given it a try, so, at the age of sixteen, I followed in my Dads footsteps and became an apprentice Bus Mechanic for West Midlands Passenger Transport, after all, it had served my Dad well for thirty-nine years so why shouldn't it do for me. I completed my five year apprenticeship and stayed on as a so called skilled craftsman for a further two years before becoming fed up of dirty fingernails so I changed direction completely, embarking on my current career in the Materials Handling industry starting as a Trainee Fork Lift Truck Salesman.

I first met my wife Kerry in 1977 at school when I was twelve and she was eleven and in the year below me. At our school in West Bromwich, I had a blinding crush on her, following her around the school like a shadow. In my mind, I looked like John Travolta; trouble was, to every one else I looked like John Merrick with the finesse and style of a greased pig on a marble floor. I always stood back in the schoolyard and looked on from afar never having the courage or the wisdom to do any thing about it at the time, so... we simply stayed friends for our remaining years at school before drifting apart. We were reunited in 1986, five years later when I was twenty-one, full of wisdom, and now with the added benefits that alcohol brings in terms of courage... I finally asked her out. She agreed and we eventually became a couple getting engaged later in the year. In the autumn of 1988 we bought our first house together in Nottingham settling down to start a family. I have always enjoyed the great outdoors and the occasional extra bit of outdoor adventure whenever it should present itself to me. Back in 1992, I was very happy it had to be said, I had a house with Kerry and we had a daughter Ashleigh who was two years old. I was always extremely happy with my lot and never craved or desired for much more, happy being a family man who goes to work and takes a holiday once a year to get my adventure, but one day, one fateful day when an open mouth and a lapse in concentration changed all that. Having spent a few years in sales and marketing I have never been one to fall for any obvious marketing or advertising blurb that seeks to lure vulnerable people in, and always prided myself in being able to spot it when it should arise, but one day I fell for it..... advertising,...... bloody advertising.

There I was sat in my future mother in laws house in 1992 with Kerry, Ashleigh and the future in-laws, all enjoying the film *'Back To The Future'*, when in an advert break they had the ad that would change everything for us. The plane takes off with a few squaddies on board, all sat facing each other getting ready to make a parachute jump, after a few nervous looks, the young soldiers jump out and drift to the ground like characters in a James Bond movie, one of them turns to the camera and gives cheeky grin before the slogan, *"TA Soldier, Be The Best"* is thrown out with the freephone number for the Territorial Army. Harmless enough you might think, but then I said it, it just slipped out...I never meant anything by it but once you have said it, it's out and there is bugger all you can do about it.

*"I wish I'd have joined the army when I left school, I reckon I should try that, what do you think?"*
Kerry seized the opportunity and came straight back at me

*"You in the Army! You wouldn't last five minutes, not only are you too old but you're not fit enough either"*,

To me it was the red rag and bull syndrome, Oh how everyone laughed. I was gutted, I then spent the second half of the film convincing the family how fit I thought I was and why at twenty-seven, I still had what it takes to make a soldier, all with my tongue firmly pressed into my cheek, safe in the knowledge that the moment had passed, I had redeemed myself, but, being at least a couple of pounds above my ideal from one too many business lunches, knew that, yet again, she was she was probably right too.

Later on as the film progressed with Michael J Fox just about to propel himself back into 1985 with the aid of a De Lorean and a 1.21 Jigga Watt Flux Capacitor, the adverts came back on with the same cheeky faced smiling squaddie drifting back down to earth. This time she was ready, not a moment wasted, Kerry leapt from her seat and produced a notepad and pen, taking the free phone number, calling my bluff, and challenging me, in front of my future family, that, if I was so fit, I should phone the number there and then. I was trapped, what could I do, I had verbally cornered myself and had no option if I was to save what bit of credibility still remained.

Not long after, I was stood with my heels together and my chin in the air on a frosty morning in the middle of a drill square at the Royal Engineers Training Regiment, Gibraltar Barracks in Camberley for my two-week recruits course, being screamed at by some steely eyed, chisel jawed Drill Instructor who didn't seem interested that I sold forklift trucks for a living, crunching his way across the square in his studded boots that sparkled like black diamonds. After less than 20 minutes of my first morning on a drill square I had already encountered the Drill Corporal on no less than three occasions, the first during our initial inspection.

I stood bolt upright on the front rank waiting as I could hear his boots crunching along the rank as he verbally crushed everyone in his path. The poor guy three to my right was pushing out press-ups like his life depended on it for the heinous crime of having a small piece of fluff on his beret. I stood there waiting my turn and shaking like a shitting dog in the park. I could smell the stale cigarettes on his breath as his nose butted up to mine, *"What's your name"* he asked softly, I knew immediately that this was part of his usual routine,

*"Woodhall, Corporal"* I replied confidently

*"Am I hurting you Sapper Woodhall?"* he asked very calmly and quietly, provoking my obvious response

*"No Corporal"* I replied

Playing right into his hands he bellows *"Well I should be hurting you seeing as I'm stood on your shaggin hair... get it cut before the next parade"*. You would have thought I looked like Billy Connolly the way he was carrying on but even before he had finished his little outburst I knew that I would begin my marathon press up regime that would last for the next two weeks. A few minutes later and with my arms still aching we are now marching across the square all trying to impress with our arms flying like a whirling dervish and feet stamping in a fashion that even Michael Flatley and the RiverDance team would have been proud of. He calls the squad to a halt; we all come to a bumping stop in a 'none military' fashion. From behind we could all hear those boots delivering that haunting crunch that had already began to instil the fear of Satan through every fibre of our bodies.

I imagined that in Canada somewhere... there must be a lot of bears, and a few of them must have sore heads.

———————

Now, according to my way of thinking, when a bear with a sore head wants to use a cliché to highlight a bad attitude... I picture them talking about a *'Drill Corporal with a sore head'*

No one knows who has upset him on this occasion but I just got that feeling that, yet again... it was I.
*"What's you name?"* he bellows storming up from behind grinding to a halt at my shoulder
*"Woodhall Corporal"* I said getting that déjà vu feeling
*"Have we already met?"*
*"Yes Corporal"*
*"If you don't swing your arms higher you and me will fall out, do you understand?"* he asked, I knew he wanted me to fully understand.

Minutes later I am marching with my arms swinging so much I'm almost producing electricity.
*"HHAALLTT"* he screams as we all bump into each other like the starting line of the London marathon
*"What's your name?"*
*"Woodhall Corporal"* I said now getting confused with his line of questioning, thinking, you might be great at drill but you've got a crap memory.
*"What are you doing you bazzerker, you nearly had his eye out... are you taking the piss? Get him off this square now!"* he screams, passing me on to his mate
*"Take him to the guard room for an hour"*
I remember thinking *"thank God for that, I'll get an hours sit down locked in a cell. I know I'm not going to have enough time to make a wooden birdcage or dig to safety, but at least I can escape Mr Personality for a while"*

How wrong I was, I emerged an hour later covered in sweat and snot loosing half of my bodyweight and hardly able to stand up having just undertook more physical exercise that an Olympian in training.

I vowed then to never re-offend and comply with every request he put to me from now until the day I die.

After two weeks of hell, I returned home a stone lighter and a Soldier, at a very basic level admittedly, but a soldier non-the less, with an Army number and enough green kit to open a government surplus store. The point of irony to this element of babble is that the position of drill instructor was the role I would play in the future armed with equally as many woven tales of rhetoric, ready to be delivered at a moments notice... with the overall objective being that of helping recruits to march in a straight line, bang their feet in unison and achieve the same level of precision, accuracy and uniformity that you could see on a Thursday night in any Line Dancing club in Tamworth.

It took me a while to fully understand, but one of the many things I enjoy about the TA is the eclectic mix of people that it attracts. It seems to me that the people with regular low-pressure jobs in Civvy Street enjoy the new found sense of power and authority that they get from being a Sergeant Major in the TA. Each person leaving behind the lack of worries and stress from landscape gardening and embracing the military role with open arms. On the other hand I know of many people who join the ranks, to start at the bottom and like it, because during the day they already have enough responsibility and authority and are looking to enjoy the other end of the spectrum and not have to think too much. A software director of a multi national company in the week, flitting between Nottingham and New York, and a Corporal at weekends... jumping through hoops of fire to please his Lollypop Man come Staff Sergeant. All very surreal indeed, but, each to his own. I spoke to one guy who was a welder by day and a Sergeant Major in the TA, he told me how the first thing his wife would do if he got his mobilisation papers would be to rush out and buy a new dress because he earns nearly double in the TA as he would in civvy street.

On the other hand, there are a few young and recently commissioned Officers who are sometimes a law onto themselves. Some are students, living in digs getting up at the crack of noon whether they need to or not, few of whom have a job... and even fewer who actually want one. Their personal life could be total chaos and without structure, but here in the army they are playing the role of a well rounded and very disciplined individual who sets an example to all of us 'lower ranks'. Each young officer chases the desire to command and manage people. At nearly forty, I do struggle with this on occasions knowing that I am taking instructions on life from someone who is younger than some of the socks in my wardrobe.

The majority of the British public and the Regular Army for that matter grossly misunderstand the TA and the important role that it plays in the make up of today's British Army, especially since the Governments Strategic Defence Review a few years back. Whenever you mention to someone that you are in the TA, his or her first reaction is to laugh, then to stereotype you, thinking that you just smear your face in animal droppings and creep through the bushes after dark playing soldiers. The TA has always had a terrible press and is likened to programmes such as "Dads Army" and has also been mocked by the media with programmes such as 'All Quiet on the Preston Front', which aired a few years back. If there is ever a TV programme where they wish to portray the character as a geek, they normally say he is in the TA. What the TA does offer the regular army is the vast array of skills that come fitted as standard from the job that they do during the day such as a doctor, an electronics engineer or a quantity surveyor. They all offer something to the make up of the British army.

For the next eleven years I would do as most other TA soldiers do and attend one drill night per week and one or two weekends a month, fitting this around a full time job, three children and routine house maintenance that never seems to end. Most people don't realise that the TA get paid the same as their regular army counterpart, taking rank and qualifications into consideration. For most, the incentive to regularly attend comes in the form of a tax-free bounty payment of over £1,300 at the end of the financial year provided that the training requirements have been met, that includes attending a two-week camp anywhere, ranging from Ripon in the UK, USA or even Ascension Island. So for most TA soldiers they have never spent more than two weeks away from home before, this was to be slightly longer than that.

Kerry and I stood in the kitchen discussing the implications of the impending mobilisation and agreed, there has never been a good time to go to Iraq in the last twenty years, least of all now as there are escalating attacks against the CF (Coalition Forces) out there, and furthermore, the enemy no longer wears a uniform nor drives a tank. Kerry was extremely upset at the thought of me going away but she knew deep down that I had to go. If you wear the uniform, spend eleven years training to do a job, when the time comes, you must do the job, it's that simple.

There was one missing piece from the jigsaw, one key issue that needed resolving prior to my mobilisation... we were still not married.... We have known each other for twenty-six years, we have been engaged for over fifteen years, we have three children together, we have a mortgage that would pay a top Premiership Footballer for two weeks work, but we just never got round to getting married, and, I was always afraid that I couldn't give Kerry the wedding she wanted and God only knows, after all these years, she deserved. We would always laugh when someone would accuse us of being afraid of commitment because we never got married, We would always say *"If you want to see commitment, come and walk a mile in our shoes and pay our bills for a month, then you will see commitment"*

But the fact remained, we were not married and Kerry was not recognised as my next of kin, should anything happen. The following Monday I sat at my desk at work and made a few telephone calls to get the ball rolling. Now I know some brides spend over two years organising, planning and preparing every minute detail of their wedding, and then on the day it pours with rain and ruins it all. I organised a Church, Vicar, Reception, Photographer, Honeymoon and my wedding uniform in under four hours, all the rest, I thought, are just minor details. I even checked a long-range weather forecast and that looked good as well.

At this point Kerry had no idea of my plans. I sat down to make the call. In hindsight, maybe I should have waited until I got home and did the one knee thing with a ring of some sort, but in my mind at that time, I had done all that fifteen years ago. I just needed to know that she would be free at 3.00pm on the 8th June, exactly two weeks from now, so I made the call from work and got her on her mobile phone. The conversation was short and the answer was yes. I didn't stay on the phone long enough to get a detailed reaction followed by a long discussion, but from the initial reaction, it was good. It seemed to me that the obvious choice would be to have our eight year-old son Alex as my best man, with our daughters Ashleigh, now twelve and Georgia age six, as bridesmaids. During the brief telephone call we agreed that I would sort out Alex and Kerry would sort out the girls in terms of what they wear. My telephone call to a military clothing shop based in Chatham in Kent who were sorting my uniform out, led me to ask if they could make a full set of 'Number One's' for an eight year old, identical in every way to the uniform they were going to supply me, and after telling them the story they took up the challenge and agreed to do it, although they only had just over a week and a half to make something that they had never done before in that size.

During the initial phone call, I said to the owner, Barney, *"Can you make sure it will be smart enough to wear at a wedding without it looking like a fancy dress outfit"*

There was a pause as I listened, knowing that I had issued a provocative statement, Barney said *"What do you do for a living when you're not in the TA?"*
*"I sell fork lift trucks, why do you ask?"*
*"I'll tell you what"* he said *"I won't tell you how to sell forklift trucks if you don't tell me how to make military uniforms!"* His point was well delivered clear and concise, I knew then that whatever he produced would look good.

Kerry filled the next two weeks with the minor details that I had missed, a wedding dress, bridesmaids dresses, flowers, guest invitations etc., although I did get involved with the small thing of buying a couple of wedding rings. We did discuss the dress code for all the guests at the wedding as being plain white Tee shirt and jeans, so people would not have to worry too much about what they had to wear at such short notice. This back fired on us when a close friend stated that she had already bought her dress, no pleasing some people.

The day arrived; Alex and I spent the night in a hotel following the tradition of not seeing the bride on the morning of the wedding. His uniform was absolutely amazing and was an exact replica of mine, accurate in every way, Royal Engineers buttons, peaked hat, gold lanyard and Corporals tapes, he was even adorned with miniature medals, his boots were like the black diamonds I saw eleven years ago, he looked amazing, it crossed my mind that he could even upstage the bride, I wouldn't be too worried if he upstages me when the photos are being taken, but the bride, that's a different matter. I had no idea what Kerry or the girls would be wearing. Standing at the alter, I saw them for the first time and they nearly took my breath away, they all looked stunning, God only knows how Kerry did it in the short time she had, but she did it and did it well.

Kerry with Ashleigh and Georgia

The wedding and reception afterwards was everything we had hoped for, our friends and close relatives attending the ceremony, with more people turning up outside the church to see us afterwards. The reception was a meal in a quaint restaurant in the next village with our close family and friends sitting down for a three courser. I delivered my speech pointing out that I had kept every one waiting for years and years and then have the audacity to give everyone only a few days notice that we were getting married, thanking everyone for being there and finishing off by thanking Kerry for waiting for me as I fought back the tears, I then handed over to Alex the young best man who leapt to his feet and climbed up onto the seat of his top table position to deliver his speech.

Alex was told of his obligation to deliver his Best Man's speech and relished the opportunity. Prior to the wedding I gave Alex plenty of coaching from how to stand up straight with his chin in the air and his chest out to giving him some guidance as to the type of things usually said in a best mans speech. I have taken his script and printed it exactly, word for word: -

Georgia on her way into the church

*Ladies and Gentlemen*
*Thank you to the groom for those kind words*

*Firstly I would like to say how beautiful the Bridesmaid and*
*Maid of Honour looks,*

Someone called out from the back of the room, *"I bet*
*that sticks in your throat Alex"* commenting on the fact
that he has just paid his sisters a compliment. A rare
thing considering Alex is of the age where he thinks it's
his job to inflict pain on his sisters.

*And finally how stunning my mummy, the Bride looks.*

*It is traditional for the best man to tell some funny stories*
*about the groom, but he has told me that if I embarrass him*
*too much he will stop my pocket money............ But I*
*don't need money...... I'm only a kid!*

*So here goes*
*The groom was born in March 1965*
*and was... lets say, ...... erm....* (he pauses for theatrical
effect)
*I can't think of another word for it   -  FAT baby*
*at over 12 pounds,*
*Now that's heavier than me when I was 4 months old,*
*And he has carried on growing ever since,*
*...even now at 38, he carries on growing*   (with this Alex
put both hands to his front and shakes his belly)

*I would like to point out that my daddy is on two diets at*
*the moment, because he says that he doesn't get enough to*
*eat from just one...*

---

*As you are all aware Phil and Kerry have known each other for 25 years, and have lived together for over 16 years.*
*I think my mommy deserves a medal for putting up with his snoring and trumping for all that time*

*And I am sure that my sisters Ashleigh and Georgia would agree with me when I say that we are very lucky to have two parents that love each other so much and are so happy together. Although it does get a bit tense some mornings trying to get us all off to school.*

*So back to tradition*

*Ladies and Gentlemen: would you please be upstanding and join me in a toast for my mum and dad, the bride and Groom*

*Ladies and Gentlemen:*
*now I would like to read out some of the cards*

*Finally I would like to wish my daddy good luck in Iraq and hope you don't get hurt.*

*I would like to wish my Mummy and Daddy all the happiness in the world, Ashleigh, Georgia and me love you both very much indeed.*

*Thank You*
He then picked up his glass of coke and said
*"To the Gride and Broom"* gentle laughter and tears excused his slip up as everyone stood up with charged glasses.

---

He climbed down off the table, having succeeded in not only delivering what would have been a superb speech for an adult, let alone an eight year old, he also succeeded in reducing every member of his audience to tears including the waitresses who didn't even know us, they just stood at the back of the room drying their eyes discretely.

The whole day was a fantastic success. Two years to plan a wedding, who needs that long, you only need four hours, a telephone and a couple of weeks to tie up the loose ends. Luckily on our wedding day not one person said "it won't last you know!" We were very lucky to have such wonderful friends rallying round to help out on this unusual belated shotgun style wedding. We had friends that organised a cake, decorated the reception room in advance of our

Alex with the ring

arrival, we even had someone who I hardly knew turn up to video the whole thing, giving us the video as a wedding present. Kerry told me that in the morning, as she was almost ready to leave the house, she noticed that the lily in her hair looked a little out of scale compared to the size of her head, in short she was wearing a trumpet just above her right ear. Panic and tears ensued quickly followed by a phone call to Pam, a great neighbour who lives opposite and who was just about to leave for the church herself, now getting in her car, touring the shops in the village looking for something that would be more suitable and less symphonic.

It appears to be the small things that are done by true friends that seem to make all the difference, allowing you time to focus on the job in hand... getting married

This is my family, Alex, Kerry, Ashleigh and Georgia

and enjoying it. We were whisked away for our two-day honeymoon in a beautiful country house hotel in Nottinghamshire, no kids, no phone, no pets, just loads of champagne and good food, enjoying each others company in a way that newly weds do. The days passed quickly both knowing that in three days time the newfound elation would end and we would be saying goodbye for a long time.

With the short honeymoon now over, the reality started to kick in, and it kicked in hard, we only had a couple more days together before going, we filled them eating out during lunchtimes and going for long walks together, but in the background the cloud hung over us both drawing ever nearer. During my time in the TA I have trained to do many things but I have never trained either in body or mind to spend long periods of time away from my family, neither has Kerry been trained to cope with our three children, two part time jobs and the school summer holidays to get through on her own, and finally, no one has trained our children to be without their father. It was going to be a testing time for us all.

During these last three weeks people have often asked me the question *"are you looking forward to going to Iraq?"*

This question I always found impossible to answer on the basis that I didn't know exactly where in Iraq I would end up, what I would be doing when I got there, who I would be doing it with or for how long, and finally, but the most important, how much I would be paid for doing it? How you base a decision on that I'm not exactly sure!

## MOBILISATION DAY

16ᵗʰ June 2003

The day has arrived and my bags are packed. I took the kids to school this morning, walking the short distance to their primary school, fighting the tears all the way trying not to get upset in front of the children, and doing my best to assure them that it would be OK. I took no chances and chose to wear sunglasses to cover my eyes. As we walked I forced out some conversation, all the time with a great lump in my throat. As we entered the playground I stopped and got down to give Alex and Georgia one last hug. The three of us just held each other for a moment. Alex was the first to break, with his eyes filling up immediately, *"I love you Daddy"* he said, just as

Georgia began to cry, *"Will you be back for Christmas Daddy?"* she asked.

*"I don't know Princess, whatever you do, please be good for Mommy when I am gone, she will need your help"*
I didn't want to let go, I just held on tight pulling them towards me as I finally broke and began sobbing quietly as the rain began to fall on us. Other parents around us began to move to get out of the rain; I knew one of us had to be the first to move.

With that I stood up and told them to go into school. They walked across the playground to the entrance door of the school looking back and waving every step. They both paused just before the threshold as I waved my arm telling them to go inside. They both turned away wiping their eyes as they entered the school. I looked across the playground to see other parents dropping their kids off and just giving them a peck on the cheek, they will be back here at 3.15 this afternoon. I don't know when or more importantly...if I will be back. Luke and Jack, two of Alex's mates had just been dropped off by their mum Tina, when she saw me standing looking at an empty playground, she knew what was happening today and simply said *"Good luck"*. We both walked back down the school drive together but I couldn't speak.
I returned home and prepared to drop Ashleigh off at her school in the next village by car.
Ashleigh, my eldest daughter, waited for a while once she got out of the car, trying to give herself a bit of time for her eyes to clear before entering the hostile and unforgiving territory of the comprehensive school playground. This morning was the hardest thing I

have ever done in my life and was very upsetting for us all.

Kerry and I hardly spoke as we drove to Nottingham, both putting on a brave face, not knowing what else to say and trying to keep the bit of conversation we did have upbeat so that we didn't set each other off. I fought back the idea of leaving her a copy of 'Bravo Two Zero' to read just to put her mind at rest; maybe she wouldn't see the irony of that gesture. We pulled through the gates of the barracks and followed the signs to the reception area. I hauled my kit out of the car and after a short goodbye, moved into the building to check in, I didn't want to make it any harder for either of us when saying goodbye, especially when you have no idea how long you would be apart. For a fleeting moment it crossed my mind that I may never see her again. I chose not to mention that either, I just kissed her for the last time and quickly moved into the building drying my eyes as I walked into the vast reception area. I began looking around in the hope that I would recognise someone, to my surprise, I didn't recognise a single person. This series of vast buildings formed part of a former munitions factory during the two World Wars and has since been used for a variety of other military uses ever since, with this section being totally refurbished over the last couple of years to form a mobilisation centre for reservists and TA personnel.

As soon as I walked through the great roller shutter door, a Corporal, with his kit immaculately pressed and wearing a badge with his name on, greeted me with his well-rehearsed patter.

*"Dump yer kit over there, label it up using these tags, take all your documentation including your I.D. card and passport with you and move over to that cell over there and sit down and wait your turn to be swiped into the system"*

By the time he got to the end of his little speech, that, judging by the speed he threw it out, had already said it at least a thousand times over the last few months already, I had forgotten the first bit about where to go and what to do, so, trying not to appear too much of an idiot, I moved very slowly hoping that he would throw me another lifeline. Luckily someone else came in right behind me… saving me the embarrassment of asking as he pressed play in his head and repeated the whole thing again for his benefit, this time I got the gist of it and moved all my kit into the designated area. It's amazing how much kit you end up taking, including my large Bergen full of green kit, sleep system and webbing plus a small suitcase full of civilian clothes. It's a difficult thing to try and pack for six months when you haven't got as clue what you will need.

I cautiously sat down waiting my turn,

*"NEXT"* *shouted* the clerk sitting at a long desk with a face pitched somewhere between very stern and bored out of his mind. He then proceeded to slap his hand on the top of each pile of papers as he set off into his little speech:-

*"You need to take one of them, one of them, one of them and one of them, take one of these address label sheets, stick one*

*of these bar codes on the front of each one of those forms, start filling them in now and make sure they are all completed and brought with you to the first session tomorrow morning, put this badge on and wear it at all times from now on then move into the next cell,..................NEXT......."*

He got the same blank look as I gave his mate a few minutes earlier. I collected my rainforest and moved into the next area of this former factory passing through the neatly painted wooden partitioning screens that formed the walls for the variety of cells that awaited me. On went the numbered badge, for the next three days I would be in group seven. I found an empty desk, sat down and paused for a moment wondering where to start. Around me were around thirty other mobilised TA soldiers that had arrived before me and were mostly a mix of people either staring around aimlessly, or trying to see what the next person was putting for some of the more ambiguous questions asked for,

*"What have you put for the Inland Revenue Question about your employers details? Is that the MOD or my civilian employer"* asked one guy who sat down next to me, by his soft Edinburgh accent and tweed blazer I guessed that he was a young officer with one of the Scottish infantry regiments. By now I was getting good at the blank, 'I haven't got a clue' look, he got that as his answer. It all reminded me of starting primary school, surrounded by strange faces and being asked questions that I didn't have a clue to the answers, all mixed in with a sense of nervous excitement, not knowing exactly what was about to happen. After about fifteen

minutes of form filling came the call for groups six, seven, eight and nine to move to the main conference cell for the first of many briefings. They started with the, 'why we were here' brief, followed by the 'what to expect over the next three days' brief, each time a different person came to the lectern to punch his way through something that was quite obviously very well rehearsed. The strangest thing of all was when we moved into the session for making a will. This is the first time that you get the hard shock that someone here may not be coming back, it's all very clinical and matter of fact in a way that avoids emotion totally and just gets on with it. We were all handed yet another form and a small brown envelope that was passed from front to back of the room. Then, in unison and precision, over seventy people all made a will together, following the instructions shown on the big screen in front and getting the total stranger sat next to you to witness your signature. It was then placed in the brown envelope, and under where it said 'TO BE OPENED IN THE EVENT OF DEATH' you put your name and number on it and that was that. I guessed that this was to be the first of many reminders over the next few weeks that where we were going was going was not going to be pleasant.

I have come to the end of my first day and after being shown to my temporary accommodation, I lay awake for a while to reflect. So much has happened in my life over the last few weeks. Only six weeks earlier my father was rushed into hospital having had a stroke. This caused untold stress to me to make a decision about my immediate future. My father has always been a strong man, who keeps his feelings very close to his chest, he never said how much stress he was under from worrying about me going, but I knew that no matter how much I tried to put his mind at ease, he would still worry. I called him earlier to let him know what was happening, I told him, *"Dad, don't be worried, be proud"* I am not sure what he said exactly as he still hasn't got his speech back properly yet, but it sounded like he will still worry no matter what. When I asked him a few weeks earlier not to worry he told me *"You will understand one day when it happens to Alex"* I knew he was right.

I have been away from home for less than nine hours and already I am missing my family. I lay on my bunk thinking about the next day. My mind began to run away with me thinking about Kerry and the kids and the fact that in four weeks time we should be going on our summer holidays for three weeks, all paid up and ready to go. I chose not to cancel the holiday yet just in case I should fail the medical, which is now the only way you could get out of being mobilised. On the other hand, I also know that, if I don't go on the holiday then neither will Kerry or the children. It's a big sacrifice for the family to give up a three-week holiday with nothing in its place.

Over the last three weeks I have been to the doctors and the dentist to make sure that I was fit enough to pass the medical, I wanted to go to Iraq mainly because I would regret it for the rest of my life if I didn't, missing out on the experience and not being able to put into practice what I had been training to do. I could hear myself saying to people things such as *"I nearly went to Iraq you know"* and knew that for the rest of my life I would cringe every time I said it. I also have it set in my mind that if I fail the medical for whatever reason, I will leave the TA. Medically I would only be down graded, but morally for me it would have to mean the end, as it would have made a mockery of the last eleven years if I didn't.

Few of my civilian friends can understand my reasoning for this thought process, but in my mind I know it to be the right decision in the long run. Most importantly, Kerry understands it, albeit that she doesn't like it, at least she understands my reasons. I have to go.

---

# ONLY THE SECOND DAY

17ᵗʰ June 2003

I woke up very determined this morning, I want to go to Iraq, my mind was made up, I had to go. There was still a couple of burning issues that needed resolving, first I have to make sure that the financial aspects are covered so that Kerry can still pay the mortgage and bills while I am away, it would be bad enough having me to worry about without having debts piling up as well. In short I earn more as a Regional Sales Manger selling forklift trucks than I do as a Corporal in the TA, so I need to make sure that I pass through the financial cell sorting out my pay before I pass through the Medical cell, deciding my fate. I have made the decision, rightly or wrongly that if the money was insufficient for Kerry to survive, by that I mean that I would be earning considerably less, I will have no hesitation but to action my contingency plan. I intend to limp into the Med centre and tell the doctor about my dodgy knees, the slip disk in my back and if he's still not convinced, I'll drop my trousers and see if he can find something wrong with my arse. I am simply not prepared to let Kerry and the kids suffer financially whilst I am away. I had taken the advise of my friends who passed through these doors some months earlier, by coming armed with every bank statement, household bill, and every other shred of proof needed to show that, it's not greed, it's the necessity of a family man and bread winner that is saying I want to go but don't let my family suffer as a consequence.

As the numbers were called I moved into the finance cell arms filled with all the proof a man could muster, and, a look of anticipation. It took just over thirty minutes to reach the final daily rate of pay.... and I was a happy man, the MOD could afford me. My civilian salary was matched, my homework had proved fruitful and my family will be able to eat better than beans on toast for Sunday lunch. That has just lifted an immense weight from my shoulders and I can now look forward to the rest of the cells as the day unfolds. After the finance cell I moved into the dental cell, we all sat nervously waiting our turn, everyone wishing they had cleaned their teeth after their breakfast and not before. Faces were being craned trying to reach that last bit of bacon stuck between a pre-molar and a canine. I had already taken the liberty of going to my own dentist during the last two weeks to get a check up and a filling or two, hopefully meaning this should be a breeze. A REME guy (Royal Electrical and Mechanical Engineer) from Telford came out with his checks pushed out like Marlon Brando in the Godfather, cotton wool loaded in his mouth with a hint of blood. He tried to speak

"ghuckin ghastards" he spluttered in a strong Black Country accent, as he walked out passed all of us sitting in the waiting area, this poor chap had just failed because of a decaying molar and had the choice to go home, get it filled and report again for duty at a later date, or have it pulled now. He went for the heroic option. We all looked at each other wondering what he had just gone through and whether this was a standard practice for anyone who needed a filling. He told us later that he had a couple of dentists climbing over him, the first couldn't get a grip on the tooth properly and it broke away so the other chap had a go and finally pulled it out. By now there was a lot of nervous irrelevant conversation taking place by some of the people who were staring down the barrel of a potential dental disaster.

I have never been a big fan of the dentist chair but have been enough times in my life to know a bit about everything from fillings to root canal work, I've done it all in my time but for now at least, I was orally fit having just passed and got another tick in the box, orally, I had nothing to worry about.

As the day wore on the numbers of people were dwindling slightly with people failing for one thing or another, some were happy to have failed, others were trying to negotiate a way back in. The people that said they were going to fail a medical beforehand and stated the reason that they were going to use, were... as soon as they had gone, being talked about, and not in a complimentary way. We were here to do a job that we had trained to do and this was simply the starting process.

After lunch it was the medical, this was to be the make or break for me. I had suffered with a prolapsed disk in my back about three years ago, eventually getting it sorted with the aid of an epidural and a load of steroids. I had pondered over the last couple of weeks whether I should mention this to the doc or not. I had heard the rumours that any back trouble and that's a dead cert failure. I didn't want to fail nor did I want to tell open-faced lies that could come back and bite me in the arse at some point in the future. I took my little sample bottle and yet again joined another queue in the med centre. The medical is split down into sections; hearing, sight, height and weight are all tested, then your urine is tested and finally you have the full 'drop and cough' from the doctor. During the few days leading up to my mobilisation date, I had been suffering with some flu like symptoms and spent a couple of days in bed, with my only exercise coming from regular bog trotting runs. As I sat in the queue to see the doctor having already passed through the hearing and sight tests, I heard one of the medics call out *"is there a Corporal Woodhall here?"* in full view of everyone sitting there... I said, *"Yeah that's me"*

*"Sorry mate you've failed..........., you've got blood in your urine"* for a few seconds I was stunned and a bit fed up that he announced it to everyone, as they all mentally distanced themselves from me fearing that they could also be pissing blood if they caught what

I'd supposedly got. I quickly moved into a smaller room with him, trying to understand what the problem was and why I was having a "man period", but he explained that it was caused by dehydration and there was only a very minuscule trace of blood, *"have you been drinking much water over the last few days?"* he asked, trying to understand why

*"No not really... I've been lain up in bed with the flu"*
*"Ahhh...That's what could have caused it then"* he replied.

After a bit of discussion we agreed that I would still see the doctor and see what he said, and maybe give another sample after a few more glasses of water. The doctors here are all civilian doctors, which I soon found out when I called him *"sir"*,

*"You don't have to call me sir, I'm not in the army"*.
He proudly announced. He shook my hand when he introduced himself to me, that should have been my tell tale sign that he wasn't a Military doctor. We then moved into one of the screened off areas of the med centre. It was refreshing to hear the voice of someone that didn't have the harshness of a military background, he proceeded to ask me what I did for a living, how many children I had, how did my wife feel about me going away, all the time he was talking he was also moving about my body, feeling joints and pushing my limbs into a variety of positions then jotting down his notes on his findings onto my medical form, all the time making me feel totally comfortably as I stood there in my underpants. I told him about my back problems in the past and mentioned the fact that

I had an operation on it four years ago. He pushed me into a few more positions that made me think that if he was female and I was paying for this, it could be seen as enjoyable. He then asked me a few more questions regarding my back.

*"Does it give you many problems now?"* he said

*"Only if I am standing still for extended periods of time or after carrying excessively heavy weights... you tell me of any man in his late thirties who that doesn't happen to!"*

He quickly nodded in agreement and mentioned that he had no worries regarding my back, then, after a few tests of touching my toes and stretching he asked me a couple more confirmation questions which I answered honestly, when he finally said *"sit out in the waiting area and drink plenty of water, give us another sample in about half an hour and we'll test you again, if that's OK, you've passed"*.

I moved back into the waiting area and sat next to the water dispenser, picking up one of the cone shaped paper cups that you can't put down and began to drink, and drink and drink. The numbers of people passing through the medical cell were now dwindling as the end of the day was drawing ever closer, the queues of people had now gone and I was the only person still there. My second sample was tested and it still had a slight trace and less than the first sample tested, so they agreed to let me have one last try. I was trying to work out how much water I had got through, in the end I gave up and settled for a quarter of a carboy of water, which I reckoned on being at least half a gallon. After nearly two hours of drinking I gave a final sample and sat with the doctor as he dipped the thin strip of paper and measured the colour against his chart, it was clear, so clear in fact that it was almost clean water coming out of my body. *"That's a pass, it looks like you're going mate"* he said smiling at me.

I shook his hand and got my barcode scanned giving me yet another tick in the box, I gathered up my stuff and ran to the final cell of the day, I was ecstatic, frightened and nervous all rolled into one.

All of the conversations I had been having with people since the letter had arrived three weeks ago were about whether I would or wouldn't be going and it all hinged on the financial and medical aspects, and now they are sorted. Once you've passed the medical, there is no turning back.

I moved outside to make a phone call to Kerry, she answered nervously and simply said

*"Well... are you going then?"*

*"Yeh..., I've passed"*

There was a long pause when I knew she was deeply upset, I could hear her begin to cry on the end of the phone. *"It's not forever... before you know it, I'll be home"* I said trying to comfort her as best I could, but even then I didn't know for sure when or if I'll be home, there are no guarantees in all of this. You just become the proverbial piece of shit bobbing down a river going where the flow takes you, with little or no say in your direction or destination. I agreed to phone her later with all the details, I just needed to let her know as soon as I could where I stood in the whole roller coaster process of mobilisation.

I arrived at the final cell of the day, the Quarter Masters store, I was the last one to go through as I passed others who had been through before me, each one walking out with a new large kit bag full of goodies. The store consisted of a 30 metre long, chest height serving counter with shelves and shelves of neatly packed desert coloured stuff. I moved first to the clothing store counter to get my desert combats, socks, Tee shirts and boots and the essential floppy hat. The Lance Corporal thrust a piece of paper in front of me asking for me to fill in the blanks on my sizes. He then wandered off into the aisles with his eyes glazed over having repeated this process hundreds of times already. Even though I was the last of the day and he could already smell the beer of the NAAFI drawing him ever closer, I made sure that each piece of clothing fitted me perfectly as there was no taking it back next week because it chafed a bit.

In addition to the obvious kit that I knew I would get, I was also issued things like a headscarf; sweat rags, sand goggles and even sunglasses. Now... when you think of army issued sunglasses, you think of the American 'aviator' style that was made famous by films like 'Top Gun', making the individual look like a sexually charged stallion, these however were more like Roy Orbison glasses with a tortoise shell frame and would only make you look like a welder, not exactly what I had in mind. I got issued a jungle sleeping bag and liner, a mosquito net and poles to fit onto the camp cot bed that I'll get issued when I get out there. Finally I was issued my weapon, the SA80 that will now be by my side for a while to come, along with the weapon comes a few ancillaries including four magazines a cleaning kit and "OH MY GOD" a bayonet... sweet Jesus, what am I supposed to do with this...all I can hope is that I never have cause to try to use it.

On day three, and after another night in the sauna of a barrack block with thirty or so other blokes we moved into a large hanger for what was to be our final cell at Chilwell. We were now in the transport or movement cell. This is where we were checked, checked again, all ready to be put on a coach destined for Grantham for the first phase of our training. Everyone fought with their baggage trying to do their best not to lose anything. Most people had come with a suitcase or two plus their webbing, but now we are armed with our new huge black army issue holdall with a shed load of other kit not to mention your new best friend called SA80. I got all my kit under the floor of the coach and, nearing 1800hrs, finally dumped myself halfway up the coach next to a guy in his mid thirties who looked at me and gave me the *"alright mate"* nod that you often give when you have never met but are forced to sit on a seat that seemed hardly big enough for two kids let alone two blokes with baggage and rifles. I looked out of the window as we pulled out, you could almost hear the sighs of relief from the staff that had been processing us for the last few days as they now handed over responsibility for us to someone else. They had taken us from the street and done everything from, make sure we will be paid on time and into the right bank account, to making sure we have the right size boots and a weapon that works. There are many things that the army does very well and processing and organising people is one of them. I was very impressed over the last thirty-six hours or so.

After a bit of 'to-and-fro' chatting it transpired that the chap sitting next to me was married with children and lived in Suffolk working for a VW dealership. We chatted freely about our families and finally both admitted to each other that we were shitting ourselves. He introduced himself as "Mac" which was short for a Scottish surname that I forgot instantly but all I needed to know and remember was that his name was Mac, we seemed to understand a bit about each other and that he was my new mate. For the first time, I was not alone.

The coach arrived through the gates of an Army Barracks just outside Grantham in Nottinghamshire; this was to be our home for the next five days. We were immediately transferred through into the gymnasium that had been converted into a reception and dispersal hall with matting placed over the wooden surface to protect the floor and a series of tiered seating all staring at a projector screen and primed ready for another well rehearsed welcome brief.

The Regimental Sergeant Major started with the rules of his camp, keeping his presentation very short and punchy using some of his well rehearsed jokes and anecdotes that made every one laugh but left them with no illusion that... if you tried to escape, then yes, you probably would get fed to the dogs or a similar ill fated end. He gathered from the minimal response from his audience that, it was getting late and everyone was exhausted from a very busy day. The final task consisted of us getting detailed to our accommodation block. We all stood in the hall and queued before three small desks to be handed a small slip of paper that had the block number, room number and finally bed number, of our new home. This, we were told... could not be deviated from. Once again we moved outside lugging suitcases, webbing and all the new Gucci kit the QM has issued us with earlier, armed only with badly photocopied map trying to find our block, in the dark through a maze of buildings that all look identical. We were in what the army call *'Transit Accommodation'*.  In hotels there is the star rating for what you can expect. In the army there is rank structure that determines your room, the facilities and what you can expect. If you are an officer you may get a touch of carpet or even your own room, as a sapper (the Royal Engineers equivalent of Private) it's pretty basic, with hard floors and limited facilities, then below that you have 'Transit Accommodation', basic, tattered, very well used and rarely comfortable. After a great amount of confusion, from countless squaddies wandering around armed with their slip of paper and weighed down with enough baggage to make even the most hardened of Himalayan Sherpa cower under the weight. Eventually we found home, a two-story pre-war brick built block with heavily painted walls, small corridors and room numbers slapped on each door, which, had been painted many times over during its lifetime, all very plain, featureless and not very welcoming. My room was upstairs and along a small hallway. As I bundled my way through the door hauling the first of my luggage having opened the door, I stood at the threshold looking along the bed spaces and knew then that the next five days were going to be a bit impersonal to say the least. The room consisted of seven double bunk beds on each side of the room with a measly two feet between each bunk and only eight metal wardrobes between twenty-eight blokes, each with a minimum of four large bags. I looked across to find where I would be laying my head that night, hoping for a quiet bottom bunk up the far corner, where I could create my own little piece of sanctuary. No such luck unfortunately, I was to be placed... through the door, second bunk on the left on the top.

I stood there for a while looking at all the kit and wondering where the hell it was all going to go, below me was a guy who had already got his kit unpacked and claimed the chair beside the bed. Bastard...... this was already becoming territorial and he had what I wanted, a chair.... a bloody chair, a piece of moulded plastic, the type of thing that if you had one in your garden you would throw it out, but here it was different... it had value... it would have been somewhere to put my towel, my toilet bag, somewhere to call my own piece of space...somewhere to sit, somewhere I could come home to at the end of the day... Now I'm pissed off!!

I made a small neat pile of kit at the foot of the bed. The leaping gazelles that were the first in the queue to get the accommodation slips had snapped up all the wardrobes and they were the ones, unpacked, undressed and returning from their first shower whilst I am still flustered, sweating and... to make matters worse, without a chair. I began to unpack my kit into some semblance of order trying to keep my personal admin well organised, when something struck me. It crept up on me without knowing, I was surrounded in a room full of Scottish lads who were all from the same infantry regiment and they never stopped talking, boy could they talk, all in fluent Jockannese. The whole speed of delivery with everything they said was completely new to me and it all seemed to be in a different language to the Scottish dialect that I had grown to know and love from films like Braveheart and Brigadoon. (Tongue in cheek). I looked round to see if there were any hind legs off donkeys following their discussions. They wanted to discuss everything from how they were going to wear their floppy hat to how great they were at playing the bagpipes. The air was filled with some of the most mindless drivel I had ever heard.... what they were going to do when they got to Iraq, how they were going to organise their kit, what clothing they had had bought and why. They all seemed to have bought into it wholeheartedly, while I was still locked in civvy mode and already missing my family, trying against all the odds, to get settled for the night. I couldn't help thinking how undignified I must look at thirty-eight years of age clambering onto the top bunk of my bed wearing only my underpants in a small room with twenty-eight other blokes. Eventually I managed to sort myself out and get over the chair envy issue from earlier and lay down for my first night in our new surroundings. With the lights off I looked forward to a well earned nights sleep, although any hopes I had of sleeping was crushed by two Scottish warriors on opposite sides of the room having a loud discussion as to who was the greatest martial arts actor of all time, was it Bruce Lee or Chuck Norris. They then went on to debate every film and each sequence of each film trying to outdo the other in their battle for oriental film supremacy. All we needed now was for Grasshopper to come in and kick the shit out of the pair of them so that we could all get some sleep.

A series of alarm clocks all chirped their tunes at varying times of the early dawn stating that, it's now half past dark and time to get up. This is where we all discovered one of the other joys of transit accommodation that is packed to its capacity, we were in one of two, twenty-eight man rooms on the top floor with only six sinks and four toilets between fifty six men. I now entered a new phase in my life, queuing for nearly half an hour, still only wearing my underpants and flip flops, awaiting a sink, all the time looking at the artwork of a lifetimes worth of tattoo's covering every inch of everyone's skin, I glanced down at my pale painting-less body and wondered if it was worth all the pain and money to look like Michael Angelo's ceiling. I stood and listened to the early morning chorus of bodily functions from the crowd around me, noises and smells being created naturally from each and every orifice and wondering to myself, *"I wonder if I would look out of place if I went and got my respirator?"*

The day was laid out for us with a series of lectures to help us when we get over there, sitting through lectures on everything from mines awareness to Nuclear, Biological and Chemical warfare. If there was anyone sitting in the audience that wasn't too worried about going at the start of the day, soon had their minds changed with the viewing of some hard hitting videos about what chemical or biological bombs have been used in the past including one involving Saddam and the fairly recent genocide of his own people. The mines awareness brought home the real threat of anti tank and anti personnel mines that are ever present in all areas of Iraq giving us all just something else to think about prior to and during our stay.

The next morning I wasn't going to get caught out with the queuing for a sink routine so this time I got up at 0500hrs, over an hour before anyone else, I had my wash and shave, and then went back to bed for a cheeky one hour snooze before getting dressed to start another day, whilst everyone else stood partially naked in the dawn chorus of flatulent nakedness. During the course of the next five days we endured a variety of other training sessions and kit issue until we finally had one thing left to do before we were fit for theatre. Injections, and what appeared to be loads of them, all the usual stuff like yellow fever, cholera, typhoid, with the option of taking the anthrax jab. All the pros and cons were thoroughly explained through a couple more briefings and, rightly or wrongly, I chose to have it. Any past horror stories that have come from the experiences from some of the soldiers who went through the first gulf war in 1990-91, suffered because of the alleged cocktail of injections given in one go. Here we were given a choice of the anthrax jab, which lets face it... is the one that most people were concerned about, plus the injections were spread across a time frame with boosters over the next twelve months. My big fear has not been with having the needle, but the embarrassment of passing out in front of a load of hairy arsed squaddies, all with their shirts off waiting in a queue. It took me back to the pressures and horror stories of the dreaded TB jab during my comprehensive school days. I also chose not to mention the fact to anyone in the queue that I almost passed-out during the skin test for the TB jab when I was thirteen. Deep breathe and look away, that is my plan. Luckily for me it worked, my injections were in and I was still conscious...a result.

We then moved on to sit through a very interesting lecture about the history and pastimes of Iraq and the various types of Muslim cultures within. This was very professionally delivered in the military theatre style conference room. This is one of the few occasions where you get to sit in a comfortable chair and let the information wash over you. The officers delivering the lecture are obviously well aware of the tired mental state of their forced audience so they introduced us to their incentives for the audience to stay awake during both the lectures and the film clips. They were armed with a super soaker water gun, with a soaking range of thirty feet that would be deployed at any unsuspecting victim drifting into a slumber as a result of the dimmed lights and warm comfortable surroundings. Next they had large plastic water filled storage boxes with apples floating in.

*"Anyone falling asleep will get a blast with the super soaker to wake them up, for anyone re-offending you must come out to the front and bob for apples sticking your head in the plastic box".*

I was one of the first into the lecture theatre so managed to get on one of the soft arm chairs at the front, I fought my way through the first film about Iraq's long history when I felt the jet of water hit my face,

---

*"Ooh ya bastard!"*, was the shocked response that came out of my mouth as I had drifted off and forgotten where I was.

*"That's, Ooh ya bastard... Ma'am"*, came the reply from the female Captain armed with her weapon of mass humiliation. There was over one hundred people in the theatre all pissing themselves laughing at my expense, but I have to admit, even I found it funny. This was to be only the first of my water borne experiences, as... within less than twenty minutes I would be out the front with my head in a bucket coming up like a pig at a banquet with an apple in my mouth.

Our final cell was where our kit is weighed including weapon and helmet with the total target weight being 55kg; any excess weight is to stay behind. A 'Married Families Overseas' (MFO) box is a large cardboard box that each person is issued with for the purpose of dumping your excess kit in. In each individual's box people were dumping all the stuff that will obviously not be needed when we get there. I left a fleece, jeans, shoes, trousers, leather issued gloves and my own sleeping bag. I got a large white envelope and wrote on it with a permanent marker pen, *'Welcome home you slender sun-tanned handsome bastard'* all in the hope that when I finally get back...I would be! The box is then checked off by one of the movement staff who issued a receipt for what is in there, finally sealing the box down with your name, rank, number and parent unit written on all four sides. This box will now be sent back to Chilwell and held in storage awaiting our return.

---

At the end of the week we were then split down into our smaller groups, Engineers, logistics, Infantry etc. We were also issued with our final documentation and certification stating that we had covered all of the training necessary to enter Iraq.

At the relevant time we were then called forward to a waiting coach whereby our large group of over two hundred had been reduced still further to a group of fourteen Royal Engineers. I now started to feel I stood a chance of getting to know some of these guys a bit better. We were counted once more and checked off against a list to make sure we got on the right coach, only now did I get the feeling that we were on our way, well, to our new parent unit at least, we were now on our way to Ripon.

From left to right, Me, Ossie, Mac and Billy just having had our kit weighed, our MFO boxes now packed. This was the last day we were in green kit for a long while.

We then endured another two weeks at Ripon going through a series of fitness tests and weapons handling tests before the day was announced. We fly on 10th July 2003.

We left the barracks at 0500hrs and set off for Brize Norton on the coach. As we pulled up to the airport I typed a generic text message to my family and friends letting them know that it was today that we fly out. I sent it to around a dozen people. It was obvious that some people then forwarded the text on to other people because I received more messages of goodwill back than the number first sent out. It gave me such a lift as the text messages of well wishes came flooding back. The time had come.... Philip Woodhall, who is, sitting on the autumn side of thirty eight years old, a

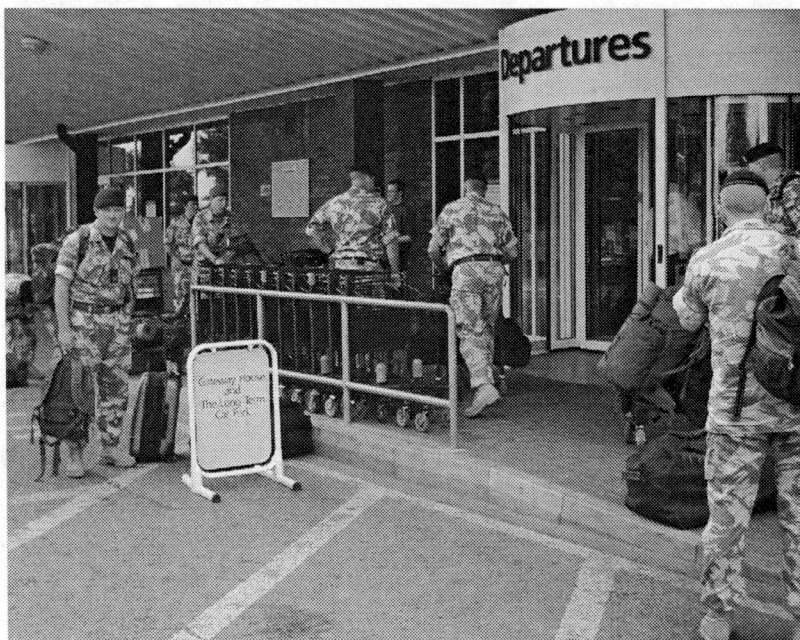

Ready to depart from RAF Brize Norton

husband, father of three young children, former Bus Mechanic, Forklift Truck Sales Manager, the very man that once opened his big mouth eleven years ago to a bloody TV advert, is going to Iraq as a soldier... God help us!!!!

# TALES FROM THE DESERT

## 11th July 2003

**W**e finally landed at just after midnight local time after a 6½-hour flight. When we were on the flight it hit us as we flew over Baghdad by night how big the place is. I turned to one of my mates and without saying a word, we both pulled a face that said, "*Oh shit, we're nearly there*". This is getting serious now, all the laughing and joking had stopped, no one said a word, and each had their heads filled with their own thoughts. As we neared our destination we were straining to see out of the windows as we landed, the lights of Basra were far greater than I had expected. Basra is a big place.

The first thing that strikes you as you leave the aircraft is the heat. At first I thought it was the back draught from the engines, but you realise when you are standing in the terminal and nowhere near the aircraft that, no, it's actually this hot. You will have experienced similar when you go on your holidays first getting off the plane. This was after midnight and still over 45 degrees. When we got into the main terminal, something struck me, all the looting that had taken place shortly after the conflict, in particular the marble floor had been completely stripped from the arrivals area leaving only the under matting that it once sat on. We stood around next to the carousel waiting for our baggage to arrive when someone gently reminded us that 'we' are the baggage handlers. *"Hurry up and get them bags unloaded, this ain't f\*\*kin Gatwick you know!"* said one of the soldiers who was working in the airport. This was the first experience we had of doing any kind of manual labour, working in the heat with nowhere to cool down. There were boxes of bottled water everywhere to just take and drink, then came our next shock, drinking hot water. The water was hot, not tepid or even warm, but hot... hot enough to make a brew with nothing more than a cup and a tea bag.

After much waiting around we had a couple of 'welcome to Iraq' briefs then finally we were 'swiped' into theatre using our ID cards, before moving into the main reception area of the terminal. This was still intact. It was all very overstated, gold effect lined everything. There were large chandeliers hanging high in the ceiling, an ocean of marble seemed to adorn everything. A few of us moved outside for a cigarette and a change of scenery, when we noticed a bit of the local wildlife.....Ants...not the cheeky little happy go lucky, work hard, play hard ants we get in the UK, but the great big one inch long type that say things like *"what the f**k you staring at"*, the type of ants you would see only in a Sci-Fi movie. We had been stood outside for a while chatting about the wildlife and trying to make sense of it all when we heard our first burst of gunfire, probably locals just giving us a warm welcome to their country. We were then quickly moved inside, the whole group stood looking at each other wondering what we had let ourselves in for.

After a two-hour wait, always standing, as no one was brave enough to upset any of the wildlife, we then... at 0200hrs, boarded a coach and were given an armed guard south across Iraq and into Kuwait. At all times, the curtains on the coach were drawn and the interior lights were off, I kept peeking through the side of the curtain trying to catch a glimpse of something, but there was nothing to be seen other than desert and darkness. There was no conversation, people either slept or sat in darkness gathering their thoughts.

After a couple of hours travelling we moved off the metalled roads and onto a track finally arriving at our camp in Kuwait to begin our acclimatisation phase of training. The coach lunged as we moved onto the soft sand parking area. By now we're all knackered as it's 0400hrs and we haven't slept in over thirty hours. From what little I could see in the darkness, it's not a welcoming place, there are lots of marquee style tents, line after line of them and nothing else. The sweat poured out of us as we unloaded our hoards of kit from the coach and moved into our bare tent about two hundred metres away, having picked our way through the lines of the other tents and trying to dodge the guy ropes.

Someone came in to give us another quick info brief, clothed in the obligatory shorts and flip-flops, before issuing us with our camp cots and rushing away back to his own tent to salvage what he could from his nights sleep.

The camp cot is a wonder of modern science being the simple camp beds first used by the American Army. Without the instructions there is now fifteen camp cots in a variety of assembly states strewn along the marquee's walls. No one quite knew how to get the last piece into place and gave up with the thought that a good nights sleep would be achieved from only three poles being in place missing out the final piece. I quickly grabbed a cot and looked for the best position,

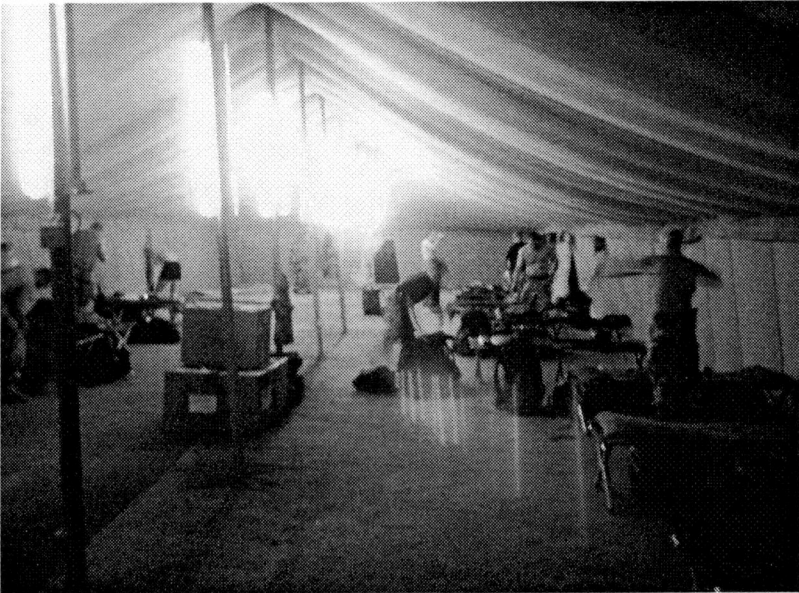

First night in the tent, my bed is the first on the right

the four corners of the tent had already been taken so I went for a position next to a side door. After a twenty-minute wrestle with the bed I welcomed myself to the fourth of what I expect to be many more bed spaces during this tour. With this incredible heat...sleep was going to be difficult. I stripped and chose to lie on the top of my sleeping bag on my camp cot with just my shorts on and a hand towel placed under my head.

The next morning I had a lie in till 0800hrs and woke to find that I was covered from head to foot in sweat and sand, my eyes were stinging from lying on my back and small pools of sweat were forming in my eye sockets. I then discovered the first of many lessons about sleeping out here.

1   Don't leave the door open if you sleep next to it. The breeze is welcoming but with it comes sand, and lots of it.
2   Don't get in your sleeping bag as you will probably drown in your own sweat or even worse suffer from heat exhaustion in your sleep, that is, if you're lucky enough to get any sleep.

I managed to drop off by lying on the top of my sleeping bag, but still found it very uncomfortable as the nylon bag becomes very wet and the sand sticks to your skin. Tonight I will try a different method, just shorts lying only on my towel.

The first job of the day is to get answers to the other two of the three most important questions when you are dropped off in any location. I already knew where I was sleeping, but I still had to find out where do I eat and where do I shit.

After a day of doing nothing other than lying on my bed and sweating profusely a few of us decided to head off out to explore what was around here. We were told about the Internet booth outside the camp about a mile away. With very little else to do, four of us ventured out to see what we could find.

**This is the first email I sent to Kerry**

*Date:*        *11th July, 2003.*
*Subject*       *Tales from the desert*

*Hello my darling wife,*

*Well we arrived eventually at a camp in the middle of the desert in Kuwait, all big marquee type tents. The heat is unbelievable. Last night it was so hot I couldn't sleep. At the moment it is around 50 degrees C and the winds are very strong, so strong in fact that you can't go out without facemask and sand goggles on, this is the most inhospitable place on earth. The sand storms are so bad the visibility is only about 100m at times; you can't see the sun at all. Some of the tents have air conditioning and are OK, but we can't use those as we are here to get acclimatised. The trouble with air-con is that at some point you have to go outside again. This is our first day so it's a bit of a shock to the system.*

---

*I'm now in an Internet booth, which is a small portacabin that is about a mile from the camp and in the middle of the desert; we get here by a small bus that is laid on for us, but I think we will have to walk back.*

*Last night we had the doors open in the tent to try to keep cool, when I woke up this morning, I was covered in sand from the storms in the night. We will be here until the 19th July just getting used to the heat and the conditions before moving into theatre in Iraq.*

*The showers here are excellent, the cold water comes out hot and the hot comes out boiling, it feels great after a shower but after two minutes you are soaking with sweat again.*

*Other than that everything is fine and it's just a case of getting used to it, I am not too worried and the morale is very good. Anyway, enough about me, how are you?, how are the kids bearing up, have they forgotten about me already?*

*We are allowed to be on for 20 minutes each time so I had better keep it short. Please give a kiss to the kids and let them know I am OK, nothing to worry about.*

*All my love my darling*

*You remain, my love, my life*

*Phil*
*XXXXX*

It's very difficult sending an email like this home because I wanted to inform her about what is happening but at the same time I don't want to give her anything to worry about. After typing this email I then sent a similar one to my dad, then another to a work colleague when... it came to me. Instead of sending lots of emails all saying similar things, it seemed a good idea to send one generic email to everyone in my address book and maybe spend a little more time on its content. I agreed with someone at work for her to forward my email to all the people that I work with. From now on, I turned myself into a bit of a journalist, reporting what I saw, bearing in mind that I couldn't give anything away for security reasons, but include enough information to keep people interested.

These emails were sent to a number of people including family, friends and work colleagues. It pleased me to know that my emails were being read by almost one thousand people across the UK, and that's not counting anyone who sent the emails on to other people. From now on I had something to occupy my mind while I am out here.

I would receive emails from time to time from people who I had never met and did not know; this helped me tremendously with my sanity.

The remaining pages are taken from those emails...

# BANDITS

14th July 2003

Today is going to be a particularly difficult day for me as it's my daughter Ashleigh's 13th birthday, the day when she changes from a lovely little girl into an acid spitting bitch vixen from hell with enough lively hormones in her body to fuel a small African village.

The day was filled with me thinking about what she is doing and what I should write in a Bluey that would help to prove that I was thinking about her. The bluey is a thin blue letter come envelope that is for the armed forces and forms the basis of family written communication wherever you are serving in the world. Before I left home I asked Ashleigh what she wanted as a special birthday present in advance of her birthday, a present that she could keep and would think of me whenever she used it. Ashleigh decided that she wanted two rats as pets!!. Thanks...

Following a dash around the pet shops we bought two baby domestic rats and a cage that would be big enough to house a couple of medium sized refugees. She seemed happy and I was safe in the knowledge that I wouldn't be there to have the fear or trouble of looking after them, or gathering them from the cat's teeth should they escape their new metal caged haven.

The next few days crawled by with the three highlights of the day being breakfast, lunch and dinner. The days could be passed a little quicker with frequent trips to the cookhouse where we play cards. In the small card school were some of my best pals all of whom were in the same predicament, having left a family, left a job, and been thrown into this surreal world of heat, fear and boredom. Ossie is a tall black guy who is among the nicest guys you could ever meet. At forty-seven he was among one of the older guys in the unit but he has a string of past experiences from the regular army that he could draw upon. The love of his life is his wife Julie. At every opportunity he would discuss what she had been doing back home. He always referred to her as *"Me Julie"*, Without any prompting, a sudden chorus of Ali G's mid chart pop song of the same name would be sung, unfortunately it's the type of song that people only know the first line to, and it quickly fades out when we run out of words. Billy was a guy in his early forties and is as plain talking as they come. You always know where you stand with Bill, he is armed with a fantastic sharp sense of Northern humour and wit so fast that you could cut yourself with ease if you are on the wrong side of his delivery. His civilian job was a HGV driver and his military job was a plant operator. It would be fair to say that fitness was not high on Billy's agenda and probably took an even footing with space travel and basket weaving as a part of his daily life. During our testing phase at Ripon he tried negotiating with the P.T.I. (Physical Training Instructor) before, like all of us, he was tasked with the B.P.F.A. (Basic Personal Fitness Assessment), with all credit to him, after the second attempt he passed...just!

Kelly was from Newcastle, and at twenty-eight knew how to handle anyone trying to take advantage of the fact that she was an attractive woman in a harsh, and some would say, *"man's world"*. In her past she has served for seven years in the Royal Logistics Corp as a regular soldier before joining the TA and already has a tour of Bosnia under here belt. She seemed to deal with all this Iraq stuff with ease and never got to the moaning phase that most of us had passed days ago.

Mac, whom I met on the coach on the way to Grantham was the world champion at sleeping, he had the amazing ability to sleep through the ferocious heat of the day and night, waking only to eat or join in with the card school.

Finally there is Elvis, he picked the name up some years ago, apparently as legend has it, when he turned up on a parade with sideburns hanging down the side of his face, and, when he was asked if he could sing either 'hound dog' or 'love me tender' to the rest of the squad, he asked why, looking back in a fearful state of confusion at the Sergeant who replied,

*"Oh, I'm sorry, I thought you were sent here as an Elvis impersonator, so if you're not the official Elvis look alike, GET RID OF THEM SHAGGIN SIDEBURNS!!"*
From that moment on he had gained the nick name of Elvis, however, instead of shortening the offending sidies to the appropriate length as stated in the Queen's Reg's bible of right and wrong, he decided to buy a pair of the classic Elvis sunglasses complete with the metal sides and increasing sized holes along the arms. These, he then wore everywhere. He was also known for not giving a damn what he says or to whom. During our training phase in Ripon we were lined up on parade waiting to be greeted by our new Sergeant Major. As he walked out, Ossie stood out front and called us up to attention. After we all sprung to attention in a bid to make a good first impression, we are told to stand at ease and relax by the SM.
*"We're Engineers here, not Guards... just relax guys"* he said.
At this point Elvis who is a Sapper (the Royal Engineers equivalent rank of a Private) decided to walk over to him and shake his hand saying:
*"Cheers for that mate, we're the TA you know... any chance I can borrow yer bike cus I could do with a piss and the bogs are miles away?"*

He got back a look of total disbelief, as everyone in the squad stood quiet waiting for the impending verbal explosion... when, and probably for the first time ever, the Sergeant Major was totally speechless. As anyone who has ever had anything to do with the army will tell you, a Sergeant Major is armed with a plethora of amazingly quick witted reply's that he has gathered over the years and ready to be deployed at a moments notice, not only putting you in your place but also sending out a signal to everyone else saying: I'm in charge here, don't over step the mark'. On this occasion, the best he could muster in the circumstances and the startling yet unconventional approach from Elvis was a simple   *"f\*\*k off!"*

Although short and effective, it wasn't the cliché filled rhetoric that we have all grown to know and love from a good Sergeant Major. Something more befitting of an experienced SM would be along the lines of:

*"Bike means fail... fail means Jail...  and Jail means you... off you go..."*
Not quite the same really. On this occasion, he was lucky.

No prizes for spotting Elvis on the front row (far right), Billy is next to him with Ossie and Kelly in the centre. I am in the centre of the rear row with Mac to my right.

In the cookhouse, which was yet another vast marquee tent, with the key difference being that it had large air conditioning units spaced along the walls, we would sit around playing the simple card game of Chase the Ace, a game which in normal surroundings would only last at the very most half an hour before boredom kicks in, out here we played it every day for two or three hours in a single sitting, all helping to pass the time and get the next two weeks out the way. The fact that the cookhouse had air-conditioning units only helped to bring the temperature into the low 30's, but it was respite from the temperatures that lay outside waiting for you to emerge once more.

One day through a complete fit of boredom from chase the ace we decided to go out and seek things to make our life a little more bearable, searching through the many vast empty tents that had been recently vacated by the units that were here before us, prior to them moving into theatre in Iraq. Others may call this stealing we called it necessity. Three of us set off in search of whatever we could find, a bungee here, a clothes peg there; it was all going to be useful. We all needed washing lines etc.. Coat hangers were plentiful so we gathered them all up to share when we got back to our tent. I managed to find a large plastic crate and a plastic chair, now this was luxury. I relished the thought of other people suffering the same plastic chair envy that I had already experienced in Grantham.

I knew then, my day would come. In one of the vast tents, still empty as it was awaiting another squadron to arrive, we came across a small pile of mattresses, a few furtive glances were thrown back and forth but we had made our minds up, we agreed that they had our names written all over them, at this point we didn't care, in our sand goggles and face masks who would identify us. We had become bandits. If, back in the UK you were to find a pile of used mattresses somewhere, there wouldn't be a snowball in hell's chance that you would even touch them, let alone take them with pride and sleep on them. It was another telltale reminder how your character changes in circumstances such as these. We clambered across a skip with excitement and anticipation, like a child on Christmas morning opening his presents. I found a pillow, a dirty...hideous... brown flowered pattern...sweat

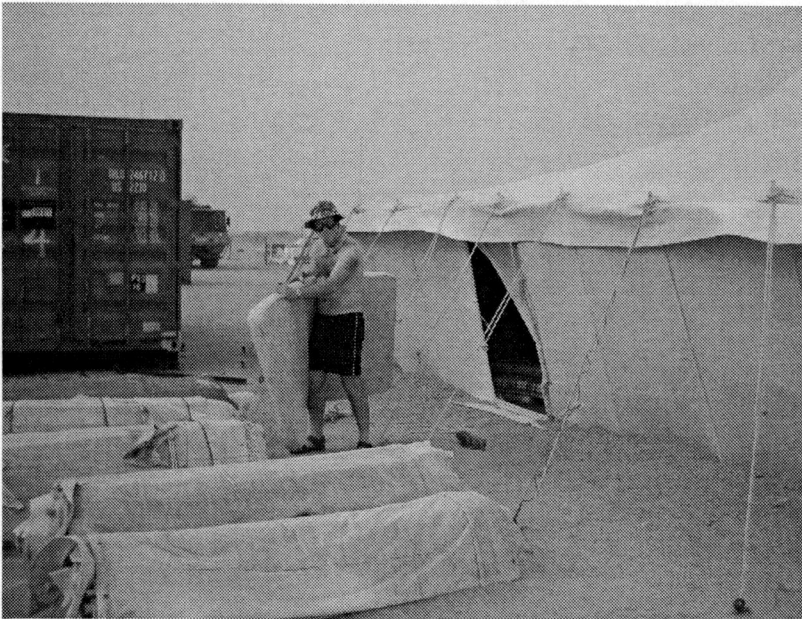

stained...dusty pillow. I could smell the stale sweat that erupted from it as soon as I moved it from its resting place...Fantastic! After a good wash and a towel as a pillowcase... it meant comfort and luxury for the remainder of the tour. I felt like Jack the Biscuit... I had what other people wanted. My stained pillow became an instant status symbol.

We came across a large industrial fridge in one of the vacant tents, standing over six feet high and four feet wide with glass front sliding doors; it looked like the answer to our prayers. Exited...we rushed back to our tent for some back up to carry the chilling beast.

Six of us returned looking at this huge fridge; a quick test lift was executed.
*"Hands on...lift...up"*
Up she went, now standing over eight feet in the air as it moved slowly across the tent.
We neared the exit door to the tent when Mac spoke with the voice of reason, *"How are we going to get this out of this tent and 200m across soft sand back to our tent in broad daylight, without getting spotted?"* It was as if someone had just metaphorically slapped us around the face to wake us from our criminal sleepwalking. We didn't want to agree with him but we quickly all agreed and placed the fridge back in its original position. We would have to continue drinking hot water for a while to come. The water from these fridges were packed so high and tight that the fridges couldn't cope with the heat that all the bottles produced, and were never in there long enough to cool before they were taken out by someone. A standard policy of 'take one out and put one back' was adopted.

---

If you managed to get a cool or even cold bottle, keeping it cold was also very difficult. The method adopted for this was to take a pair of standard issue desert combat socks, thick long and woollen, stretching them both over the bottle so that it was now giving an insulation layer. Then completely soak the socks in water. As the water evaporates from the socks in the heat, it draws away the heat from the bottle, thus creating a refrigeration effect. Again, it's surprising how creative people become when they need to be.

Later in the week we were getting a bit fed up with drinking hot water so we did a recce of the cookhouse after dark. Bingo... we had not only come up with a source of cold bottled water but it was frozen. It was then that the seeds were sewn for the perfect crime. Three of us set off after dark armed with one head torch, ten bottles of hot water and some cigarettes. Mac and Billy would approach the cookhouse tent smoking a cigarette trying to look inconspicuous, as soon as the coast was clear, the signal was given for me to scurry under the flap of the tent, and the two lookouts then rolled the hot bottles of water under the tent. I then moved the hot water into the freezer under the guidance of my coal miner's style light fixed on my head and took out ten bottles of ice for the boys. The whole process was then reversed for the getaway. We had the ice and by morning so would the chef. Everyone's a winner! We carried on this well drilled procedure every night that we were at that camp. The more times we did it the better we got.

During the daylight hours we received various training to assist us in theatre. We had lessons on a variety of subjects including, driving in Iraq, Mines awareness, the history of Iraq and its cultures. I never knew, for example, that Iraq was under British rule up until 1929. It was also the home of the Hanging Gardens of Babylon. Iraq is a country steeped in history and tradition, however... the media has only reported the worst aspects of this struggling nation, its leader not here to support the man in the street. The following months will allow me to understand further their plight.

We also had a lesson on foreign weapons and how to clear them should we come across someone having to remove it from them and clear it, making it safe. Weapons recently seized were spread across the sandy floor of the marquee, ranging from the all too familiar Kalashnikov AK47, to the home made rifle constructed using a long piece of conduit tubing as the main barrel and a small nail as the firing pin. The rifle butt was fashioned from a piece of wood using thin tin plate and nails as the securing medium for the whole weapon. Very crudely made but demonstrating amazing ingenuity considering their limited resources, also bringing home the reality of the extreme lengths that some people are going to, to defend themselves and kill.

We even received lessons on the ways to avoid the 'Camel Spiders'. We were told that they are called 'Camel Spiders' because they climb onto the bellies of camels and eat their stomachs from the outside, numbing the flesh by secreting a natural anaesthetic.

The camels don't even notice until their intestines fall out, they run over 25 miles per hour, they make squealing noises like a child screaming when they scamper about and worst of all, they live and take shelter in the comfort of the chemical toilets.

This was then followed by an officer demonstrating to the group, his five point plan on how to avoid a camel spider hanging off your dangly bits whilst going about your business in the small plastic Tardis of much redemption.

1 *Before opening the door, rock the whole chemical toilet building from side to side.*

2 *Open the door and then slam it shut three times making as much noise as possible*

3 *Once inside, give the main body of the toilet a further two kicks*

4 *Using your boot, lift and slam the toilet seat at least twice.*

5 *Drop your trousers and your dump as quickly as possible, just in case the banging never woke the critter but the smell did!*

From that day onwards it added a certain something to the daily visit, always keeping you 'on your toes', especially after dark as this is when they were said to be most active.

As time went on there were no sightings at all in or around the tent and camp, did these beasts really exist? Or was it simply a legend, like the Loch Ness Monster or the Beast of Bodmin Moor. As the days went by there were reported sightings but still no evidence, each time bringing your anticipation and fear of these Goliath's of the desert ever higher. Last night in the wee small hours, I lay awake mopping my sweat when I heard a scratching that seemed to be coming from under my bed, in the darkness, I reached for my head torch and then turned it on to reveal a camel spider the size of Gloucestershire making its way from my bed across the tent. Human nature took over at this point as I screamed like a teenage girl at a Boy Band concert. Quickly realising that I was supposed to be a rough tough soldier, I announced its presence to the sleeping occupants of the tent by turning the main fluorescent lights on as my heart was racing so much that it affected my voice to now have a strange warble. Immediately there were more than twenty people leaping about in various states of undress and tiredness, not all people were pleased to find four large fluorescent lights turned on at 3am.
*"Oi...turn that f\*\*kin light off you twat"* echoed from the far end of the tent

Most people instantly got up curios to see what all the fuss was about. I was just hoping that, when it was finally caught, it was as big as I had first thought and more importantly, big enough to save my reputation. Everyone wanted to join in, but no one wanted to go near it as we had heard so much about these beasts, but never actually seen one. Its speed was unbelievable, across the floor, up the wall and then onto the inside ceiling of the tent, all at the same incredible turn of speed. Finally the Scottish Corporal who had earlier shown his annoyance at the lights being turned on finally climbed out of his bed and cornered it and after he introduced it to the underside of his size 10's, he paraded his catch on the table for all to see.

*"Now can we get some f\*\*kin sleep"*
No one slept soundly last night.

Now curious to find out more about these gargantuan flesh-eating monsters, I wanted to find out if these things really do lie in wait ready to eat your knackers at their every opportunity, I decided to do a bit of research on the internet. Here's what it said;

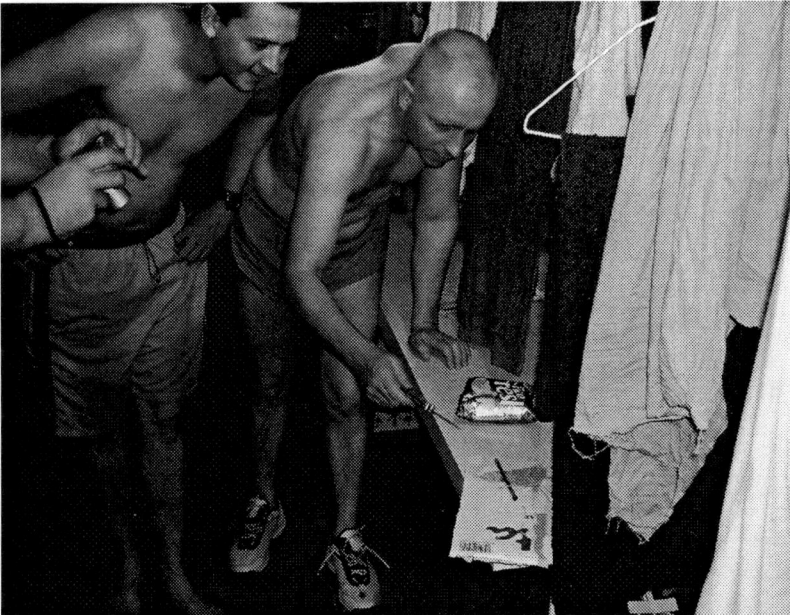

The spider being paraded on the table, difficult to see in this shot but it was huge...honest!

*Camel spiders are one of the fastest running arthropods growing as big as an adult hand. Although they have four pairs of legs, they run using only three pairs. The first pair of legs or pedipalpi are held up in front of them and used in a similar manner to the antennae of insects. They have very long, silky setae and are constantly moving in order to locate and pick-up prey. Despite their fearsome appearance and their strong bite, solifugids are unlikely to harm humans. In the past they were considered venomous and extremely dangerous but it is now thought that the only risk of injury resulting from them is caused by shock or infection following a bite. There is no evidence of venom in any part of their body. Camel spiders are nocturnal predators of other arthropods including scorpions and are voracious feeders. Some species kill and feed on lizards and it is speculated that others kill mice and birds. They rely solely on their speed and stealth to catch their prey. In desert areas they are often attracted to lights at night in search of food and their appearance can cause alarm if they enter tents. It is rare to see them during the winter months and they are thought to hide or hibernate during cold periods.*

Not one mention of gonad munching or taking your leg off and carrying it away in the night, but still enough I felt, to keep you on your toes in the chemical toilet. I will still use the five-point plan every visit.

More to come...

# TALES FROM THE DESERT PART 2

## 19th July 2003

Since my last message I have spent eight days doing the 'Get used to the heat' thing in Kuwait, basically sit in your tent and bake, not nice, the temperature at 5.45am is over 100 degrees, then during the day it warms up another 40 degrees. People are telling me that you will get used to it, to me that sounds like shit, how anyone gets used to temperatures like these I don't know.

Since then I have now moved from the Kuwait acclimatisation phase and crossed the border into Iraq. What an incredible transformation. The borderline is a vast cavernous ditch stretching at least fifteen to twenty metres across and ten metres deep. This vast channel carves a divide across the landscape separating the two nations. As we passed the checkpoint border control it changed from being almost normal to seeing the total devastation that these people have endured. As we moved towards Basra, it got worse. All the buildings have been bombed to devastating effect. It's very easy to spot an Iraqi tank; they're the black ones upside down with holes in them. At all times you are under armed guard but you still can't help thinking, "is he the one with an RPG". (Rocket Propelled Grenade), We are hearing about contacts every day from the troops coming back into camp who have been out either patrolling or escorting. This starts to play on your mind, as you know that it's a lottery when you go out of the gates. Another of the sights that first grabs your attention when you cross the border are the signs everywhere saying *Do Not Feed or Throw Food to Children*. As a father I struggle with my conscience when I see kids as

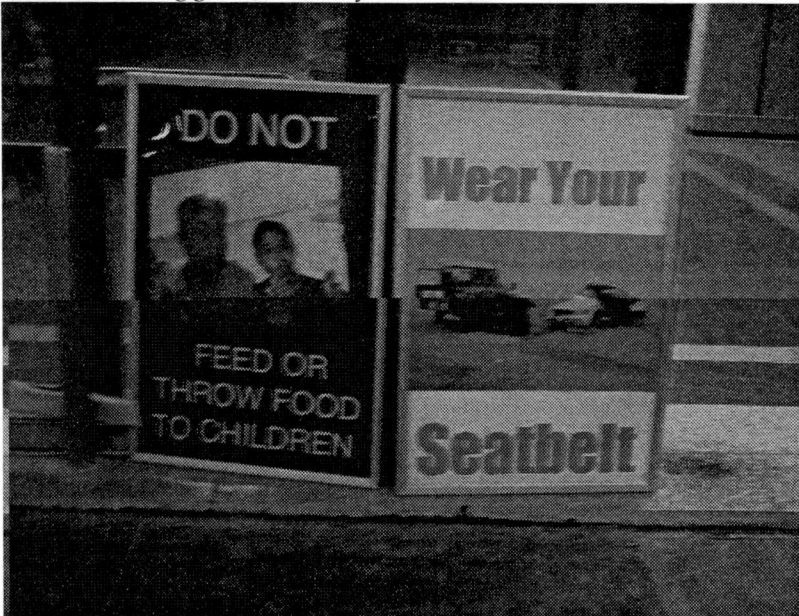

young as four wandering about in the desert roads, standing in front of traffic trying to stop you and beg for food and water. This could be lethal for them as they dodge and weave through the traffic, or for us, as they are also sometimes part of a trap you get you out of your vehicle positioning you as a sitting duck for someone else to take a shot at you.

I am now based in a place called Shaibah Airfield about five miles outside Basra. This is an old Iraqi Airbase that was taken over earlier in the year. As we entered it we were waved in, I can only struggle to imagine the firefights that took place by our boys earlier in the year to take control of this area. I know that I have it easy, but it doesn't make it any easier. As we departed the transport I felt the same as I did a few weeks earlier when I was dropped off at the mobilisation centre. This time it's a few degrees warmer than Nottingham and I have twice as much kit. The coach dropped off five of us. We left the air-conditioned coach and immediately got stifled by the heat once more. Dragging our kit off the bus we said goodbye to the others who we had all become close to since mobilisation began. There was a fair bit of confusion, as we had no idea where to go or who to see. We were now in a small town made up of large tents and ISO containers all lined up to form great walls of lockable storage space. We were now going into our regular units as augmentee's. Put simply it means that we were going to fill jobs in a regular army unit and work along side regular squaddies as opposed to being mobilised as a complete TA unit, like chess pieces placed in a game that had already started. Not many regular squaddies know what we can or can't do, and most have a similar opinion of the TA as the average man in the street, that being one of ignorance. I saw a large Royal Engineers flag flying outside a portacabin with a series of large antennae filling the skyline. After a bit of chat we all agreed that the portacabin must be an Ops Room or HQ and at the very least, house someone who should know of our arrival. We dumped our kit and made our way over. The whole area was very well laid out and formal looking but in a desert army fashion. There were large pebbles everywhere keeping the dust down to a minimum with black plastic walkways laid over the top to make it a bit easier on the ankles when walking. Two plastic pathways ran parallel to the cabin office with the large flagpole in the centre marking its territory as Engineers. Two large information boards were placed outside the cabin with a variety of notices ranging from, daily squadron orders to welfare messages, like the one advertising a forthcoming Bingo Evening. Connected to the ops room cabin was another office that was the HQ for EOD (Explosive Ordnance Disposal), that's the bomb squad to you and I.

Outside their office was an impressive display showing examples of finds since they have been in theatre, anti personnel mines, land mines, grenades, RPG's etc. All giving us another reminder of reality out here.

As we made our way down the pathway someone spotted us and came out to greet us. Luckily Elvis wasn't with us, if he was to have been there he would have been first off the bus and made his entrance with something like, *"Hi mate, we're the TA and we've come to get you out the shit and help you catch the bastard!!"* Just enough to piss them off and get us all tarred with the same brush.

Instead a Sergeant who seemed genuinely pleased of our arrival greeted us as we approached the ops room. This surprised me as I was expecting the steely-eyed chisel jawed archetypal Sergeant to start screaming in their special language that only other Sergeants understood. We were all to form a part of the HQ squadron within the regiment, each of us to do the trade that we had specialised in since first joining up. This left me a bit out on a limb. All of my colleagues were looking forward to doing exactly what they had trained to do, signals, combat engineering, carpenter, and clerk. I was a bit different. The conversation went:

*"So what's your name then mate?"*
*"Cpl Woodhall"* I replied
*"yeh but what's yer name?"*
*"Woody"*
*"What trade are you?"*
*"Sigs"* (Signals)
*"Are you a class 1?"*
*"Not exactly"*
*"What do you mean, not exactly"*
*"Well"* I began *"I've been mobilised as a signaller but the last time I touched a radio was when I did my basic sigs course in 1997"*
*"Oh right"* he said looking at me puzzled
*"So what job do you do in your TA unit"*
*"Recruit Drill Instructor for the regiment"* He looked at me in disbelief,
*"Are you serious?"*
*"Yeh"* I replied, knowing that he was disappointed.

---

*"Oh F\*\*k... you're going to be a great help out here then in the desert, that's all we need... a shit signaller who teaches drill"* Clinging to a glimmer of hope that I may be of some use to him he tried his final question.
*"so what do you do in civvy street?"*
*"Sales Manager"*
*"sellin what?"*
*"Forklift Trucks"*
*"Oh sweet Jesus..............., ah well, welcome to Iraq!"* he said shaking his head. I was one of two signallers posted out here, and the only male signaller, the other being Kelly... so, I was pointed in the rough direction of my tent in the far corner of the camp. Feeling completely rejected and useless, I dragged all my kit into the tent in about four journeys and finally ended up in a tent sitting on my bergen looking around and sweating like a bull mastiff waiting for someone to turn up. The tent was empty of people as they were all out doing their job somewhere but full of their kit. The tent is an 18' X 24' standard military unit with a sunscreen stretched across its roof; it houses seven bed spaces in here. My potential bed space is currently full of their washing bags, boxes and a series of other military droppings. Washing lines were stretched across the corner of the tent where my bed should be. I sit for a while contemplating my next move. Do I move all their kit and piss them off before I have even met them or do I sit around and wait. I chose the former and moved a washing line filled with issued socks, brown T-shirts and underpants. Within an hour I had assembled my 7' X 4' mosquito net and prepared the fifth of my bed spaces, which is surprising how homely you can make it. I used a couple of cardboard boxes once filled with bottled water to provide a small

cupboard. The issued sweat rags were stretched across the surface as a small tablecloth and a lockable tin footlocker then housed my personal possessions. This acted as my bedside table with some photos of Kerry and the kids sitting on top. After a couple of hours work I stood back to admire my new home. I don't think I will be installing the surround-sound home movie system just yet but my cardboard box dressing table is a work of art. I lay on my bed for a while contemplating the last few weeks and how my life had changed so dramatically... when it hit me...there is no cooling draft inside this tent and even less inside this mosquito net, I was melting. I tried everything to cool down but it was all useless. I stood in there for about twenty minutes... I have to get out before I drown in my own sweat.

I have been told that my tour date end is November 10th, so I would expect to be home by the end of November hopefully, which is fantastic as the thought of missing Christmas from Kerry and the children would be very tough indeed. Last night I lay thinking about Kerry, Ashleigh, Alex and Georgia and quietly sobbed myself to sleep. I feel completely useless stuck out here in this shit hole. Am I cut out for this?

More to come...

# TALES FROM A FORGOTTEN PALACE

25th July 2003

Funny how things turn out really! As you have read so far, I have not been in the greatest of surroundings nor have I seen the finest of sights since I have lived out here. My last correspondence told of my move to Shaibah Airfield just outside Basra. Having spent a week there I was moved again, to the Palace, probably because they discovered that I was of no use to them whatsoever. I have now gone from the sand tents of the desert to living and working Saddam's marble palace sitting on the banks of the Shatt Al Arab River, a tributary of the Euphrates. The palace itself is not just one building but an entire village of buildings and palaces for his wife/s, sons Uday and Qsay, Chemical

Ali, the Republican guard and all of his other hangers on. There are huge ornate gates on the way into the grounds with a highly fortified wall surrounding the grounds. In the centre of it all are a series of saltwater lakes, which have been linked into the river allowing the passage of small boats etc.

The whole thing took over six years to build with Saddam apparently only ever visiting it once to open it. We were told that everyday three meals were laid on to feed him and his entire family just in case he should turn up. He never did and the food was wasted. Unbelievable really when almost right outside the gates there were people begging and searching across tips and sewers looking for anything to make their life a little better.

 The journey to get here was one of the strangest journeys ever, partly because I am just not used to these sights. Kids begging every time you stop. The motorway has no lanes or lane procedures; there are donkeys and carts everywhere. It is not uncommon for people to drive the wrong way down a motorway because it's shorter!!

SOP's (Standard Operating Procedures) is to travel with a minimum of two LandRovers, each vehicle with two people in. You must wear you body armour at all times and have you rifle loaded. The body armour weighs twenty Kilos and is very tight fitting, held together at the sides with large Velcro straps. Each time you put it on it fills with sweat immediately and its tight fitting design makes it difficult to breath in.

Currently there is a bit of mixed tension since the notorious brothers, and sons of Saddam, Uday and Qsay Hussein were killed yesterday. When driving you have to concentrate on keeping the vehicle moving at all times and not stop for the fear of the vehicle being surrounded and mobbed leaving you no escape route. The thing is, here people either welcome you or want to kill you, and they all look exactly the same!!!!

Having experienced the sights of down town Basra it's alarming to see this place for real. What we all take for granted on the news, is not the same as being here because you can't fully understand the feeling of these people, not knowing if they support you, or despise you being there. As you slowly drive through the traffic of the town, you cannot tell, as they look you in the eye which side of the political fence they sit. The tension in the air is ever present. Another aspect that you can never appreciate from watching television is the smell that fills the air. For example, you would never experience the stench of the sewers or rubbish tips, from the refuse that is simply being dumped on the side of the roads, nor do you get the rich smell of crude oil as you drive past vast lakes that have been formed by burst oil pipelines being either bombed or just damaged during the wrath of war. Everywhere you go there are smells that are as shocking as the sights. You can only feel for the people that have to live here, knowing that Basra was once, long before Saddam came on the scene, a beautiful thriving community.

---

The Palace is the Head Quarters for the Brigade, where all the decisions are made. I can only think that the decision was made from my last location to send me here because they figured that if they put me somewhere near an office with computers I might be of some help at least.

Having arrived at the palace I was taken to my new home, it's a house that was formerly one of the houses of the officers from the republican guard. I found out that I would share it with about twenty-five others. The house is one of many buildings in the grounds that form the village that is 'The Palace'

I clambered out the back of the Landrover and began to gather my kit together. I seemed to be acquiring more kit the longer I stay here; I now have the lockable foot locker, mosquito net style dome tent and a 24' face fan that I bought from the squadron shop at Shaibah. It is yet another status symbol to go with my pillow and plastic chair. The Corporal helping me summoned over a young sapper to give me a hand.
*"This is Cpl Woodhall, give him a hand to get his kit in the house and show him where everything is"*
*"This is Sapper Cunningham, he'll give you a hand"*

The young black guy who seemed to be in his late teens, put his hand out to shake mine and smiled.

*"Hi Corporal"* he said
*"Call me Woody, ...What do they call you?"* I asked
*"Jerome"* he said as he began to unload my kit out from the back of the LandRover. Jerome seemed a really nice chap who had a smile permanently fixed across his face,

he told me about some of the other guys who live in the house, and within a few minutes I knew the names of all the people who were considered as OK... and the names of the people who were considered less favourably. He lead me into the house through the hallway and into the large room at the back where a TV was on and a guy sat on a large floral patterned velour settee playing a Playstation, he looked up and to my absolute amazement said:

*"Hiya Woody, what the f\*\*k are you doing out here?"*

Two years earlier I had attended a two-week course as an instructor on a regular army barracks teaching recruits alongside other army instructors. One of the instructors was a likeable guy called Ginge Wilkes, named because of his naturally striking strawberry blond hair. Ginge was as ginger as a big orange ginger thing and as ginger as they come, and was one of a small handful of regular soldiers that I actually know well... and someone whom I considered to be a thoroughly professional soldier, well...from the bit that I knew anyway, so to walk into his house in Basra was, for me not only unbelievable but also great news. This was a fantastic breakthrough, I know someone, I have someone I can have a conversation with about way back when...someone who already knows what I can and can't do...someone who will hopefully support me with a bit of credibility and help me to loose the drill instructor come shit signaller tag. We exchanged missing details of people we knew as Ginge got me set up with a bed space on the roof and a kit store next to his downstairs. The roof is the only place where you can sleep comfortably as the houses are simply too hot to sleep in (No Aircon), (at least there are no camel spiders here) The building soaks up the heat through the day and, just like an economy 7 home storage heater, dispenses that heat out at night.

I finally felt good about where I was, as I knew someone who could introduce me to other people and make me feel welcome.

Yesterday I started my new job, which will be my full time job for the next few months. It's in the Ops room situated in the air-conditioned grand hall of the palace. The floors are all marble with vast columns everywhere, the ceiling itself is a fantastic work of art, and carved wooden shapes adorn everything, ornate plaster, hand painted in different pastel colours cover every inch of the walls. Dark carved wooden decorative panelling hangs two feet deep around the entire ceiling where the whole structure snakes itself

The ornate ceiling in the Palace

around the hall detailing out Saddam's name in Arabic wherever you look. It would be easy to get confused by the place thinking every thing around here is wonderful.

I was then introduced to Max, a Warrant Officer who is in charge of the signals side of things out here, or, 'Q Flags' as his position is commonly known. Max smiled and welcomed me to his team, I did wonder if he would still have made me as welcome if he knew how shit I was as a signaller. I seemed to get on well with Max from the outset as we were both of similar age, the main difference being, when he left school he joined the army and made his way through the ranks, when I left school, I became a bus mechanic and a fork truck salesman. We chatted and exchanged details about our lives and how they were similar. We were both married men with families with all the joys that that brings. I could relate to him and I felt...him to me.

All the other guys in the house were in their late teens or early twenties most were single or had a girlfriend. Sometimes I did struggle as I just felt like the oldest Corporal in town. If you are a regular soldier and approaching forty, you would be nearing your twenty-two year point and during that time you would expect to have been promoted more than twice.

Max passed me on to Jerome who would baby-sit me through my first shift in the Ops room. He made sure that I had everything laid out with his hand produced idiots guide for me, detailing all the important things I needed to know, ranging from how to log the incoming messages to where the hole punch was kept. I owe a lot to Jerome for today. Tomorrow... I am on my own.

Each night I sleep on the roof facing the stars, laying on my camp cot listening to the sound of gunfire in the distance, which kicks off around 10.00pm and carries on throughout the night. The nights are the worst time for me, that's when it's just me, no other distractions, nothing else to divert my attention, nothing else to think about, just my thoughts running away with me. I lie there for hours struggling to get to sleep in the heat and the noise thinking about my family, wandering what they have been doing today, wandering if I will see them again.

Each morning I am woken at around 4.00am by the sound of all the Mosques in the area, each one calling to prayer via their loudspeaker system. It takes a lot to sleep through this, so each morning I wake, completely exhausted from lack of sleep having to start another day.

The great thing about the location where I live is the view when the sun comes up across the river, how it changes the colours in the sky, the seamless gradient from jet black, through deep blue to the orange on the horizon as the sun comes up. The view from my rooftop looks across a lake and palm trees onto the Shatt Al Arab river and is quite simply breathtaking!! The background photograph on the cover of this book is taken from my bed space.

———

Earlier this morning I carried out the other part of my job out here; I was an Escort Commander for the Internal Mail system. This is where you provide an armed guard acting as a postman for all of the Royal Engineer units dotted in and around Basra. Plenty of things to tell you about... in my next email,

The hardest thing about being out here is without doubt living away from my family. I have never experienced homesickness before and didn't fully understand what it actually meant. God only knows what must be going through the minds of my family.
To say I am missing Kerry and my children is an understatement. Don't take your loved ones for granted.
I am still smiling though!!!!!

More to come...

The view from my bed meant I could watch the sun rise every day; it was a small pleasure out here.

# OUT AND ABOUT IN BASRA

29th July 2003

Since my last note I have started to get into my routine, it's already starting to feel a bit like Groundhog Day!! (It means nothing if you haven't seen the film), anyway, as I said last time, I work now in Saddam's Marble palace in Basra. My job has two roles, one is to work on the ops desk in the HQ working radios and relaying messages on the task updates happening in the surrounding Basra area. It's very boring, but at least it's air-conditioned and I feel safe. That is one part of my job. The other part is Escort Commander. This is what I do every other day, which is great as it breaks up the monotony. So in short... I have trained for eleven years with the army to come to into theatre as a receptionist and a taxi driver / postman!

All journeys have be to with two vehicles, with two people in each vehicle, all with loaded weapons and body armour, so even the simplest of tasks takes four people, even delivering a letter to someone takes four people.

So what sort of things are we doing?

Well as you probably know, the Royal Engineers build things and rebuild things as part of their role. As the region has suffered under Saddam, the CF did them no favours by bombing the place to bits; strategically this meant roads, bridges as well as military

A good example of the work of the Royal Engineers, the destroyed bridge having been replaced allowing the road to be used once more.

establishments. The regiment is split down into smaller squadrons and then troops all tasked to do various construction tasks ranging from, rebuilding police stations, constructing permanent vehicle check points to rebuilding bridges. Yesterday I spent the day going round all the various task sites to photograph the jobs for progress reports. The tasks included a bridge for a key supply route that was bombed in April, A new design of Bailey Bridge was constructed to span the damaged section, and where bombs have simply blown a smaller hole in the bridge, then a smaller 'over-bridge' is used. I also visited the site near where six RMP's (Royal Military Police) were killed earlier in the year, the Engineers are now turning this back into an Iraqi police station as one of many in the area.

We also went to a recently refurbished police station now fully up and running. It was a fantastic welcome as you walk in, all the police want to shake your hand and try to talk to you, even though neither party speaks the others lingo. *"Hello Mister"*, they say shaking your hands vigorously. One policeman introduced himself by name and placed his hand to his own chest so that I understood what he was saying. He then pointed to me with his open hand asking for my name,

*"Woody"* I said with my hand to my chest returning the gesture.

They then replied *"Aahh Woody blah blah blah ..Woody blah blah blah ...Woody blah blah"*, I then heard my name echoing around the courtyard of the Police station as around seven Iraqi policemen all started babbling and laughing to each other in Arabic with the only word I understand being my own name from what they were saying. I smiled back and looked on for some clue. Knowing my luck they were probably saying something like:

*"Aahh yes, Woody, we heard they had sent a complete toss pot to work their radios, we never knew his name was Woody... wasn't that the name of the cowboy in Toy Story? Yes... and I heard he now uses the pillow the dog used in his basket and we threw out when he shat on it...Yes that's Woody alright"*

One aspect that is often overlooked is the work that is being done by local contractors. These are Iraqi companies that have reformed themselves and are responding to MOD tenders for work that is contracted out. Most of the tendering process for rebuilding work is carried out by the Royal Engineers. Earlier today we went round collecting some of the simple tender responses from businesses for work to be carried out on bridges in the area, some of which are printed on one or two sheets of plain paper. If only we could win business in the UK with responses like that. It felt strange going into some of these so-called offices. We travelled along a series of back streets in down town Basra, leaving two people in the vehicles outside while two of us went into a small maze of buildings, all partially wrecked.

We then moved into this house and up the old wooden stairs into a small room with a very old conference table. We were given a very warm welcome; *"Hello Mister"* was the response from these old guys sitting around the table. I stood at the end of the table armed with my weapon and a personal radio attached to my ear giving us two way comms with the vehicle parked outside near the pavement, I stood silent over looking everything that was taking place. The main man sat behind the large desk at the other end of the room, his shirt was lemon in colour, open necked and looking freshly pressed. This is something you don't see often out here, fresh pressed clothing. This guy was obviously the owner and very eager to get his business back on its feet. I did wonder if the other five man sitting on the ageing soft furniture in the room were his minders. Other than the main man, none of them spoke any English, but all nodded and smiled at me eagerly whenever we made eye contact, holding out their hand with fingers parted and outstretched showing the palm clearly. The main man called out to the back room, something in Arabic, seconds later a woman in her late twenties walked in clutching a piece of paper, she didn't have her face covered as the majority of the other women do around here, but she

The waiting vehicles outside keep watch

did walk looking at the floor constantly. She didn't look at either the Sergeant who brought us here or me. I felt a bit uneasy looking at her but was curious. I also hadn't got a clue if I had just broken a great taboo of looking at a Muslim woman. She handed over the paper and moved swiftly out of the room. He then presented his proposal to rebuild a damaged pontoon bridge here in Basra. Jools, a Sergeant in his early thirties, gave me the nod and we said our goodbyes by shaking the hands of every man in the room before making our exit. We made our way back through the building and out to the LandRover's to make our way back to the palace.

"Hello Mister" is the only thing that most Chogies (Iraqis) can say. The kids on the other hand seem to have a wider vocabulary, "Give me Dollar Mister" is a firm favourite along with the cries for "water water", it took me a while to get to understand a joke that all the kids seem to enjoy playing on the British Soldiers. That is, to put their thumb up to you with a big smile as you drive past. I found out that in Iraq, putting your thumb up means the same as the middle finger means in the UK and USA, so you can imagine the fun they have when you wave back with a big grin on your face!! We would often find ourselves surrounded by small groups of children all delivering their largest and widest grin calling "mister mister, water water!!" knowing that, where there was a British soldier there was invariably a plentiful supply of fresh bottled water. Against all signs of my own human nature, we are ordered not to hand out water and open the

---

floodgates, this is sometimes almost impossible to do but you must bite your lip and give out nothing.

Two nights ago as I was lying on my bed on the flat roof, two large explosions were heard, followed by about one minute of gunfire, and then sirens could be heard echoing into the night. This happened about one kilometre away from where I lay, I felt the blast through my body as I quickly got up too see what it was. I peered from the rooftop into the darkness but couldn't make out anything. It was all happening in the distance but still a bit too close for comfort. When I was in the Ops room the next morning it appeared that there were two cars involved, they fired two grenades into a liquor store and tried to loot it. The gunfire was the locals trying to kill the looters!. Surprisingly no one was killed. There were no British Forces involved.

For us, daily life continues, even though sleeping is getting more difficult.

More to come...

## WELFARE

31ˢᵗ July 2003

Today I thought I would cover the subject of welfare, how do all these squaddies get looked after whilst out here?

Pretty well is the answer, but you do have to make some sacrifices. Firstly there are no flushing toilets, only chemical toilets (CT). Anyone who has ever been to Glastonbury knows the joys of CT's. I have discovered there is only one thing worse than a CT and that's having to use one at the end of the day following fifty other squaddies when it's over fifty degrees outside and even hotter inside...............I don't need to go on I think you get the message!!!

Showers are pretty good when they are running as the water originally comes from the salt-water river and is then treated in one of the RO Plants (Reverse Osmosis). This basically takes all the salt out of the water and makes it suitable for washing etc. These are on most camps. Showers are now restricted to one per day, not so bad as you shower at the end of the day to help lower your body temp. If you run out of water, which happens about twice per week, you get two or three bottles of drinking water and shower with those by just pouring them over your head, stood on the front garden of the house.

Drinking water. Every one needs to drink an absolute minimum of six litres of water per day to keep your body hydrated. You would think that if you drank that much water, you would be running to the toilet every few minutes, but this is not the case as you just sweat constantly. You hardly need to go, once per day maximum is the norm. Bottled water is everywhere you just go and help your self. The difficulty comes in finding it cold enough to drink, for example if you took a bottle that was just lying around and not from a freezer, you could pour it over your hand and it would almost scald you. Cold water is very difficult to find, keeping it cold is even harder. The old trusted method is still used, by taking the bottle when cold and placing it in a thick army sock and covering it with water, this helps to keep it cool for at least a few hours.

Food. The one thing you cannot complain about out here is the food, in the cook house there is a very wide choice of dishes ranging from salad to a roast lamb dinner. You can't help but feel sorry for the chefs as they are working in absolutely unbelievable temperatures, and producing meals for hundreds of soldiers, it amazes me every day how they do it.

Working around the camps doing labouring jobs are LEC's (Locally Employed Civilians) or Chogies as they are called by the British army folk. A Chogie is not necessarily an Iraqi, nor is it detrimental but is the name given to the indigenous population of the place where you are serving, wherever that may be in the world. Here, they work for the princely sum of one dollar fifty per day. Now before I hear you leap to their defence and argue the slave labour argument. The British Army wanted to pay them ten dollars per day but were warned against this as it would falsify the economy round here and create ill feeling amongst other people in the area. Basically they would become too rich, too quick!!

Contacting home is relatively simple, but like all things is monitored. As you already know we have access to the Internet at the rate of twenty minutes per day. (I often find time during slack periods in the working day when it's quiet to churn this stuff out).

You also get a phone card issued each week, which is valid for twenty minutes, the phones are readily available but you do sometimes have to queue if you go during peak times. Evenings are the busiest around 9pm here, 6pm in the UK... allowing for the three-hour time difference (GMT +3hrs). Only a twenty-minute phone call per week is tough on my family and me as it works out at, four minutes for each child and eight minutes with my wife, per week. Each and every time is very difficult because each conversation tends to start with, *"have you been good for mommy?"* and the conversation ends with Kerry in tears telling me of the things that they have done, taking advantage of her good nature. Conversation is always very difficult as I found that I couldn't say exactly what was happening as all the calls are monitored and none secure, plus the worst thing to do is put the fear of God into your wife and family. Last week I used up a phone card trying to contact the parents of one of Alex's mates who, between them had smashed a window in my garage early one Saturday evening. I obtained his number in the village where I live and called his mates Dad on the phone and only had about four minutes left on my card to explain to him that the delay on the phone was because I was calling from Iraq and that I needed his help to fix the window in my garage. Luckily he was a builder and understood my predicament, fixing the window within half an hour of my call. This is something that army does not prepare you for, the awful feeling that you get when there is an issue at home that would normally be a simple problem to resolve but because of where you are, you can do very little to help.

There is a shop onsite within the grounds of the palace which sells cans of pop, sweets etc, but that's about it. One day I visited the shop with Jerome, who...at nineteen, was very attracted by the shiny things in life, the very things that, at nineteen, and with no outgoings and loads of disposable income, you simply cannot walk away from. A multi functioning pocket knife come pliers that, when you press the knurled slider on the side, opens out to reveal a pair of scissors, a corkscrew, a toothpick, and paper shredder, a Black & Decker workmate and a small two tonne trolley jack, none of which you can do without. So with money burning a hole in his pockets, he had to fulfil his post-pubescent spending frustration whenever he could.

Furthermore, as he was very addicted to his trips to this compact little shopping emporium for his daily fix of retail therapy, today would be no exception.

*"What you after today?"* I asked trying to tap into the red mist of his spending delusions,

*"I need some batteries for the mini camera I got in Kuwait, and I like the look of these illuminating key ring torches, they are blindingly bright and only four dollars"*

I looked at the technology that lay before me and dared to press the button of the key ring to see if it was truly blinding as he had so expertly described it.

To my amazement this minuscule key ring emitted enough light to force people to begin to get up for work if pointed in the right direction. Not tempted on this occasion I parted with one dollar and bought my usual three tins of Fanta from the fridge and walked away. Jerome on the other hand stood at the till now the proud owner of a multi functioning pocket workshop, a mini face fan and a digital radio alarm clock, though what he would tune it into round here escapes me.

*"What are you going to do with that thing?"* I asked

Before Jerome had time to muster his answer the guy manning the till leapt to his defence at the thought of his loss of turnover shouting in a broad Irish accent

*"F**k off you, leave him alone... he's my best customer?*

---

A lot of people have brought out some home comforts with them such as portable telly's and Playstation's etc.. These came out in their comfy boxes that were loaded into the containers and travelled here by boat. You can sign out, from the QM's dept a DVD film for free but the trouble is you have to sit inside to watch it when the heat... as always... is truly unbearable. Electricity comes from the generators onsite and it's not uncommon to get a power cut two or three times a day. You just strap on your head torch and carry on. We also have a plentiful supply of cyalume glow sticks; these are thin plastic tubes that contain two types of liquid that mixes to cause a light producing chemical reaction when you snap them. They glow for a couple of hours and will help to create a bit of a glow but nothing spectacular.

I do my washing sat outside the front of the house. I use a galvanised steel bucket, half filling it with water and a handful of washing powder. I don't bother trying to achieve the bluey whiteness that you only get in a Daz advert... because in twenty-four hours time I will be washing them again so what's the point. The water always ends up as beige slurry with all the sand and dust that's in everything. This job is a pain in the arse because you do it everyday but if you don't let it build up it's not so bad. Washing takes about twenty minutes to dry in this heat. I tend to get my washing done before I go for my evening meal and when I return it's completely dry. You can put it in the chogie laundry system but it's not reliable. I tried this once after my first couple of days of being in theatre when I was at Shaibah, and as predicted the load with everyone's washing went missing, I lost half of my uniform for two weeks and was down to my last set of desert combats having to wash and wear every day. This was a bit of a pain in the arse but like everything else out here, you learn to adapt very quickly.

More to come...

The daily clothes washing routine. Doing this each day makes you appreciate a washing machine.

# TRANSPORTATION

## 4th August 2003

I have just got back from my driving detail around Basra on what is probably the hottest day since we have been here, and it got me thinking about the uncomfortable world of driving in Iraq. So, today I will talk about the joys and pleasures to be found when driving out here and transport used by the locals.

In the UK we take for granted things like courtesy and rules of the road, getting frustrated only on occasions if someone so much as dares to pull out on us at 30 mph. Well here in Basra there are no rules of the road; it appears to be a free for all. Yes there is a direction, i.e. they all drive on the right hand side of the road most of the time, but that cannot be relied upon. For example if you are travelling down the MSR (Main Supply Route) which is their nearest to a motorway, you often get Chogies in lorries who don't want to go over the flyover to go in the opposite direction, they simply do a U turn or travel the wrong way up a slip road and off they go.

Speed limits don't exist but it's safe to say that most of the Chogie transport struggles to top 30 mph anyway; they just chug along in their Datsun Cherry with out a care in the world bellowing out blue smoke. Obviously there is no such thing as an MOT or insurance, so you will find that often at night, there are cars with no lights at all, some have no windscreens. What you see people travelling in or on here makes you grateful for what you drive back home.

There is the other side to this, for example last week I mentioned about the work we were conducting on Bridge construction with some local Iraqi businessmen. As a part of the deal, they asked for a car so that they could do some business on our behalf. We agreed and acquired a black 735i BMW, nice car in the UK but for its age, although it probably would be viewed as a bit of a pimpmobile. Out here they refused to drive it as they said that it was too dangerous... as it meant they were probably linked with people who had too much money and potential supporters of Saddam and his cronies, So we swapped it for what?????

Two of the worst heaps of scrap you have ever seen in your life, two twenty-year-old pick-up style Datsun's. The vehicle bodywork was battered, the tyres were bald and they belched blue smoke.

They were delighted, they would simply blend in and no one would bat an eyelid.

Moving on from cars you then have the Lorries, I could write a book just on this subject alone. All of the lorries look like they have come straight out of a 60's American film. The biggest thing that strikes you about them is the fashion statement on the front wheels. They all have Ben-Hur chariot style triple headed spikes sticking out of the centre of the front wheels by about six inches, some have only one tri star spike, others have two or even three, but they all have them. Now I am sure that it is done because they think it looks good as opposed to a method of taking your legs off if you get too close. All the bonnets on the lorries have been cleaned so often over the years that most of the paint has disappeared leaving only the rusting metal showing through. In every case, the bonnet at some point in its life will have suffered some sort of bang causing dents over the paintwork, and in each case the lorry's owner will have done his bit as a would-be panel beater armed only with a hammer, a rock and loads of enthusiasm, knocking it back to something like how it should have originally looked. You can safely say with total honesty, that, in every case, these lorries, despite their age and the conditions in which they have to operate, are without doubt very well looked after by their owner/drivers. Whenever there is a queue of lorries parked on the side of the road waiting for entrance to a building or compound, they will be out with either a cloth wiping down the cab or with the bonnet up doing a bit of maintenance. When you travel along the road in the morning you will see some of the longest traffic queues ever, and they all lead to one of the two petrol stations in Basra. People will queue for over three kilometres for the very product that is produced less than twenty kilometres away. Then you have the black market petrol industry. Chogies who sit on the side of the road with a big old vegetable oil tin full of petrol. You can see them all squatting on the kerb with a fag in their mouth trying to flag down other locals in a bid to ply their trade. Other roadside businesses cropping up are three feet long blocks of ice for five dollars. I saw a kid riding a bike with a great big dripping block of ice on the rack at the back of his bike. The heat was making the ice wash away in no time as he fought his way home. I imagined he would get home with a piece of ice the size of an ice cube and a firm bollocking from his dad for not pedalling fast enough.

Another thing... that is quite surreal is sheep and goats for sale on the side of the motorway. Not in pens or anything so sophisticated, but simply wandering around munching a pile of grass that has been dumped. Think of it like a kind of drive through slaughterhouse on the motorway. People would pull up in a car and point out which one they wanted; I imagined them saying *"Would you like it in a bag or still on the hoof mister?"* It's not uncommon to see sheep just standing on the back of a pick up...I have even seen a sheep sitting on the back seat of a car with the driver weaving through traffic making his way home.

There is a vehicle that is very popular out here that I have never seen anywhere before. Imagine a pedal tricycle with three small car wheels and a pick up style flat back, a bit like what you would expect a pedal powered Reliant Robin pickup to look like.

Well...they are everywhere, ridden by kids normally hauling over half a tonne of stuff from 'A to B'. It's crazy to see them struggling to pedal as they try to keep up with the donkeys, lorries and knackered cars on the roads (including the motorways!!!!) Some are very crudely manufactured and are obviously a back street welding job using bits of metal and car parts, however, others are adorned with chrome bars around the back and wheel trims on the wheels. I guess there must be a status with these trikes as with the spikes on the wheels of the lorries. They seem to be able to carry the weight and still manage to pedal them on the basis that they have incredibly low gearing, meaning that you pedal furiously and don't seem to go very fast. I can't imagine how tiring they must be to move. You not only see them in town but miles out of town and loaded to the hilt, lord only knows what it must be like to pedal one of these over such distances across the desert roads, but they do and seem to do it well, albeit, what alternative do they have?

Coaches and minibuses are everywhere. They are always packed with people going off somewhere, always with blank faces staring out into space, the windows are open and they are never smiling, hardly surprising really considering the heat and the surroundings. Not only do they get packed to capacity on the inside, there are people hanging off them from the outside as well as sitting on the roof. Lorries have kids hanging off the back as they trundle along. Then, you have the driving style adopted by the British Soldier including yours truly. It's a bit like playing one of those computer driving games where you just weave in and out of the traffic, everyone overtakes and undertakes. If you leave a gap, somebody will fill it. It is vital when you are driving that you do not allow a gap to appear between you and your escort vehicle. The driving out here dictates that all vehicle moves are with a minimum of two vehicles, keeping the gap closed is sometimes very difficult due to the volume of traffic and the style of driving.

The method of overtaking is:-

1. A quick blast on your horn,

2. Charge through with your vehicle. When you are providing an escort vehicle, you must stay together, no matter what.

We are taught that if you ever get into any form of trouble, you must remember that you are driving you biggest weapon, i.e., use it as a means of escape as a last resort if you have to, your own imagination can fill in the missing details, never allow your vehicles to be compromised. The amazing thing is though I have not seen an accident (yet) and I have never seen anyone suffering from road rage. Basically if they smash their car up, they try and patch it up, if it's a write off they cannot claim on insurance and probably couldn't afford a replacement, they would have to move back to the pedal powered robin!!.

One final thought for when you are sitting in traffic and complaining about the heat for those not fortunate enough to have air conditioning. Try sitting in a sauna wearing a uniform and boots on, wearing Kevlar body armour over the top and with the windows shut. Not nice but a great way to lose weight!!

More to come...

# TURNING UGLY NOW

## 10th August 2003

It's been a few days since my last message, No reason other than there has been nothing to really tell you, you already know how hot it is, you know a bit about the surrounding area, and you know that the answer to all of your questions to me via email are *"Shit, Shit, Shit, and Shit"*.

So what else has been happening? I have been doing a lot more driving around the Basra area providing a guarded escort for whoever we are escorting, very often people who are considerably more important than me!

---

Yesterday I had to drive a couple of Officers to a Bridge Building competition in another squadron's location. The competition meant that a bridge made of cardboard and wooden dowelling had to be constructed to span a 400mm gap. The bridge was then tested to destruction on the weight it carried. The winning team supported over 310kg. I couldn't help thinking how much that little competition cost you and me the civvy taxpayer. I reckoned on a few thousand when you took into consideration the salaries and all the vehicles used to get the people there. There were at least a fifty people present.

Ah well at least you know your tax isn't going to waste!!!! It was a lot of fun though in an otherwise drab existence. It's vitally important out here to do anything that will help to raise morale between the

The small 'A Frame' Bridge is tested to destruction with the aid of a weight lifting bar.

troops so I agree with creative ideas like this being very important.

I mentioned in my last note to you regarding transportation that there were massive fuel queues, well this is now getting out of hand. Basically there are a few tribes, for want of a better word, in the area that are raging a war against the Coalition Forces in whichever way they can. Up until now public opinion in this area for the CF has been, in the main very good. However these organised tribes have been blowing up their own facilities affecting the local population, i.e., the power station, the petro-chemical plants, the water lines etc, generally making life for the chogies even more unbearable than they already are. This then has a knock on effect that gets the chogies to start thinking that the CF are doing nothing to stop them and then start changing the views on the population toward the CF. This situation has now dramatically escalated with riots and demonstrations all over Basra against the CF. Today I was lucky enough to be on my Ops Desk duties day in Brigade HQ instead of my driving duties day, which is tomorrow.

The Ops desk reached melt down at around 1300hrs today with me taking reports from all troops out and around in the Basra area, that they were getting completely surrounded by thousands of angry locals rocking and shaking the vehicles. As I have stated before, you drive your greatest weapon and many people found this today as they tried to escape the stoning and shooting going on around them. Four people that I share a house with, (there are now twenty nine people in our house) became surrounded and then heavily stoned with rocks by the enraged crowd around them. All of the windows were smashed and Heather, a young female Engineer who was driving the vehicle, escaped suffering a few minor cuts requiring stitches. This situation could have ended a lot worse... they were lucky. There have also been a lot of Improvised Explosive Devices, (IED's) basically home made bombs laid around the Basra area targeting CF. Four days ago two LandRover's hit a trip wire set across a dirt track regularly used by the CF. The trip wire had been set to activate the IED on the side of the road. The first LandRover not seeing the wire drove over it pressing it to the floor, but the second escorting vehicle got it tied up around the bumper triggering the device. It blew the side out of the LandRover, luckily there were no deaths but two of the people in the back of the LandRover have superficial wounds, perforated eardrums and are now completely deaf.

Are they lucky or unlucky? Both I guess!!

As of 1300hrs today there is now a total ban on all military vehicle movements in and around the Basra area. The amazing thing to me is that when I was first mobilised, the first response from people when they heard I had to come out here was always the same;

*"I thought it was all over out there!"*

Well I did as well, but there is the other side to it being, nothing gets reported back to the UK media unless it involves death, so how are you, the British public supposed to know.

Two weeks ago there was a British officer shot by a sniper with two rounds to the chest. His Kevlar body armour saved his life, but the sniper then realised that he was wearing body armour and still standing so he was then shot twice in the legs. Luckily he lived.

It was decided that this type of news does not get released to the media. But it is going on every day here. I also get the same response when you tell someone you are in the TA,

*"That's not like being a real soldier"*, is the usual response.

I will try and remember that when a chogie with an AK 47 approaches me, and I will remind him that he can only shoot me on a Tuesday night and every third weekend in the month!

More to come...

## THE DUST SETTLES...OR DOES IT!!!!

14th August 2003

Firstly, thanks to all who send me emails but as you can imagine it is difficult to reply to you all as my twenty minutes flies by and there's always a big queue. Please keep them coming...

It's ironic really that I could not produce my emails for you over the last few days to let you know what's been happening as we were suffering with a lack of power just like the chogies. Our Internet and phone facilities here have been off for a few days, hence no contact with anyone. On average we get five power cuts per day. Anyway it's on now so I'll continue....

The three or four days have been a strange mixture of heat, fear and boredom. You are probably now aware of the issues described in my last communication relating to the fuel crisis that has caused the rioting. It was very well planned indeed, on the Friday all was well, but on Saturday the signal got passed around via the hundreds of Mosques in Basra and a plan was put together. It all kicked off like lightening. Burning roadblocks and stoning were everywhere, it was not a nice place to be at all as a British Soldier.

A couple of nights ago we received intelligence to suggest that we were going to get a mortar attack on our accommodation that night from across the river. We all took our helmets and body armour to bed with us for safety whilst sleeping on the roof. I lay there on my bed looking at the stars thinking, should I go to sleep or not. There were enough helicopters patrolling that night to allay my fears. Though it was difficult to sleep with all the noise from the rotors!

The next day I was on a driving detail through the town and I am not too proud to say I was scared. During that journey my vehicle was rammed by some chogie in his 1970's Toyota, Luckily he only caught the near side rear of our vehicle. It happened at a busy crossroads. I got out of the vehicle to inspect the damage and the man started shouting something in Arabic probably saying it was my fault that he rammed us, or something similar.

I could see that this scene was quickly going to turn ugly as many Iraqi cars began to stop and circle us. A small crowd began to gather and abuse started to be directed at us so...I ordered all in my section to get into the vehicles and get away quickly. This we did to a barrage of stones and verbal abuse. That was not the place to start exchanging documents and insurance company information.

The reason they try to ram you is simple, he had two hundred witnesses to say that it was not his fault in a bid to get the MOD to pay up for all the damage to his car. Damage that had probably been there since Saddam was only a school bully!!

Driving around Basra since that day has not been the same. We were made aware that there was only a five-day truce for the CF to start sorting the electricity problems out. After that... who knows!

You can understand their frustrations when you see what little they have and how important electricity is for them. For example, all of the fuel pumps are electric, so no electricity... no fuel. The air conditioning units also require electricity. We're not talking the type of aircon you get in a hotel in Disneyland here, were talking just basic rusty old units that cool down to about 35 degrees if you are lucky. To them, that is vital in this heat.
As you drive around it's sad to see the change in attitude in just a few days. Before Saturday, most people would smile and every kid would wave and run alongside your vehicle shouting the little bit of English they know. (I had one kid shouting *"Manchester United"*. I didn't want to crush his enthusiasm by trying to explain to him that I don't even like football!!!) But now everyone is either

throwing something at you or giving you the 'thumbs down' sign. This to everyone is a clear sign that attitudes toward the CF are changing out here very quickly.

It's also frustrating for us, especially when you hear of all the fantastic work that is being done by the CF to rebuild the place. Remember we are the Royal Engineers; most of what we do is to build and repair things. There is a large Norwegian Engineer Squadron out here working with the British; they are doing some work on repairing Bridges. The bridges out here vary from fifty-year-old pontoon bridges; to Bailey bridges to new modern concrete structures which have been bombed.

As I sit in the Brigade Ops room everyday, all the Engineer tasks get reported in to me via radio so that a full picture is formed at the end of each day as to the progress of all the tasks going on around the Basra area. All of those reports are passed via radio to me from the different squadrons and I formulate them into one report that goes to the CO, (Commanding Officer). So you can imagine how frustrating it is when your vehicle gets stoned... they are accusing us of doing nothing, when in fact there are around thirty reconstruction tasks going on every day, not to mention the thousands of mines that have been cleared by EOD. If only they knew the facts.

On Tuesday I did a driving detail where I drove reporters from 'Soldier' Magazine around some of the task sites. One task was to re-erect the pylons across the desert near the Ramala Oil fields. What an enormous task. The pylons were damaged during the war with precision and strategic bombing, but since then, the chogies have continued to do what they do best. Steal!!!

In this instance, steal the copper power cables. Now we're not talking about a bit of wire. We are talking of hundreds of miles of power cable over 25mm thick and thirty metres in the air. Apparently the method used was to cut through a section from one of the pylon legs using oxyacetylene cutting equipment. Connect the towing hitch of a 4 x 4 vehicle, and simply pull it to the ground.

If there were ever to be an Olympic Games for stealing things these locals would win Gold. They are to thieving what Brazil is to football. They are quite

This operation repaired pylons previously destroyed by thieves for the copper cabling. The Royal Engineers reconstructed many hundreds of miles of pylons to reconnect the electricity supply for the people of Basra.

simply the best. I must point out that this is not through greed but necessity, as there is no B&Q superstore out here. If they see something and it's not bolted down, it goes.

One of my pals from back home is from just outside Liverpool and is a (Blue) Scouser through and through. Bobby joined the army just after Field Marshal Montgomery and has enjoyed weaving tales to me over many years of his native land on the Mersey and all that goes with life on its fair shores. He has told me on many occasions about things that disappear in the night without a trace; telling of the colourful characters that make it the place that it is. He mentioned to me on many occasions that, in Liverpool, if you don't lock it... you'd lose it. I think that it's unfair to say that it's a trait of Liverpool as most cities in the UK are like that. Here things disappear in seconds. Stuff that back home would have no monetary value or need.

Everything here gets stripped to the shell in days. As a piranha would strip the flesh off the bone they take everything until only a frame or chassis remains. For example, there are two hovercraft carcasses just sitting on the side of a runway in Basra near the former Naval Academy which have been stripped within a couple of weeks. Of what possible use a Gas turbine hovercraft engine would be is beyond me but it proves my point. Somewhere in Basra there is probably a proud chogie with the worlds most powerful sewing machine!!!

Earlier today I have completed a driving detail through Basra liasing with some local contractors.

After that I was invited along to join the CSB's (Combat Support Boats) on the river patrol.

When you have spent weeks trundling around on the shocking roads in a LandRover sweating through heat and fear, these boats are the nearest thing you could get to sheer enjoyment. They are jet boats, which don't have propellers; they shoot jets of water from under the boat. This means that they are as fast and manoeuvrable as a car.
It's the first time I have been on the water since being out here, but it was well worth the wait. You leave from the jetty inside the grounds of the Palace and make your way to the river via one of the inland lakes, then out onto the open water travelling up river past all the rusty fishing vessels. It's amazing that some of these things float but they do. Further up the river are vast ships lying on their side as we pick our way

through. These ships are the remains of the Iran-Iraq war and the first Gulf war in 1990. Each ship has a central core showing the explosion or impact; they lie across the whole of this vast river. As we near the old port of Basra a vessel named 'ALKHANSAA'. (Which is the name of a woman who converted to Islam at the time of Muhammad and encouraged her four sons to go out and carry out jihad, to fight the enemy) sits motionless for many years, with green and white IRAQI LINE livery, she lies slightly on her side exposing the now faded red coloured hull formerly sitting below the waterline with its stern pushed onto the bank of the river by the powerful flow. Only when you pass at close quarters can you fully appreciate the sheer size of these stricken vessels. As this is the first time I have ever seen anything like this, all I can do is stare in amazement as we pick our way past these immobilised hulks.

Saddam's Yacht Al-Mansur, lying on its side

Beyond that is Saddam's Yacht also lying on its side, with the name still visible *'Al Mansur'*. The vast white ship with the holes in the decks still visible from where it was bombed, showing the enormous wealth that Saddam had whilst others in the country had nothing. The remainder of the journey toured the area of the port with the docking areas housing vast Derrick cranes for stevedoring products from ship to shore with enormous lifting capacities around thirty tonnes and standing over forty metres high, again... as with the ships... motionless for many years.

After returning back to the palace two hours ago I decided that my half-inch long hair was too much and so have just been for a hair cut by the chogie barber in one of the palace buildings. He has set himself up in the large TV room in the hall of one of the palaces, a small queue of soldiers sit patiently waiting for their hair cut, and like any other salon, reading irrelevant magazines, all years out of date, and little of it relevant or interesting. Placed on the walls along side the mirror in front of the barber's chair is a selection of photographs displaying the selection of haircuts on offer. It shows a range that are all a variety of the same thing, the classic short back and sides with the only difference being the age of the soldier unfortunate enough to be caught as the model. There is even a short back and sides with a bit of a comb over side parting for the officer in the autumn of his years with a thinning top cover. Every photo shows a squaddie with a false grin on his face that says *"hurry up and take the f\*\*\*in photo as I am getting the piss ripped out of me stood here posing for you......"*

He spent thirty minutes cutting my hair. My hair is very short anyway but he was cutting it like his life depended on it. He carried on doing my eyebrows and every other bit of stray facial hair he could find, it made me realise that in your late thirties you get hair growing from most orifices on your body as it slowly migrates from the top of your head. It didn't help matters much when he proceeds to put his electric razor in your ears. I couldn't believe it, all that for one dollar, yes about 60p for a bit of welcome male grooming. I gave him four dollars and he was thrilled. It made me feel good and him feel rich. In his broken English he told me a bit about his family, his children and his hatred for Saddam, the regime and all it stood for. He mentioned that someone in his family is believed to have been executed, with no one having any knowledge of why, he quite simply disappeared without trace.

With my head now resembling that of a suede peach, I was given my final driving detail for the day. As we put on our body armour and loaded up with our weapons in the loading bay ready to move out on this routine trip, we were stopped at the gate. Minutes earlier a LandRover had been blown up in Basra by an Improvised Explosive Device (IED) and two Rocket Propelled Grenades (RPG's) I am not sure at this stage if there are any casualties but there can not be any survivors from an attack like that. It makes you realise how fragile and precious life is out here and what a lottery it is all becoming.

So here we are... our five days are up, the truce set by locals to stop the riots earlier in the week giving the CF to time to sort out the electricity is obviously at an end, and we wait to see what is going to happen tonight or tomorrow. The five-day truce was an impossible and unrealistic request to repair everything in such a short time. The tension here is immense with everyone.

On a final note, I have been granted R&R, to you civvies that's a week off. Rest and recuperation is an important part of any tour as it puts you back in contact with your family. It will no doubt be very emotional for all.
I will be flying home for a week around the 18th Sept so I hope to see you all over that period. How strange it is to be so exited about taking a holiday in you own house!!

I simply cannot wait. I hope you are enjoying the hot British weather. According to our 'five-day old' newspapers it's now 35 degrees in the UK. Ha!!!. Last night the temperature here dropped to 46 degrees.

We can but only dream of it being that cold !!!!

More to come...

## INTO THE 80's

20th August 2003

As I have mentioned in the past, it's a bit warm out here, I may have also mentioned in passing that I live in a house with nearly thirty other people with the numbers growing every few weeks as more Engineers work from here. In our house we have a communal television room, not one that shows satellite TV or anything as sophisticated as that, it has a PlayStation 2 stuck to it so that we can watch DVD's. Also in the room we have an old knackered settee and a couple of armchairs. Not the design you would choose if you were on a shopping trip to Ikea for some blue bags, tea lights and a pot plant, but a deep purple velour design with a pattern more befitting of the 1970's. However, as you are beginning to realise, for us this was luxury. Even out here there are certain etiquettes to follow when sitting on the great settee. When you sit down without a shirt on, you must place a towel between your back and the chair so that your towel soaks up your sweat not the furniture.

With boredom as a constant companion we all enjoy sitting down to watch a film, but when the entire film list has only ten DVD's on it there are only so many times you can watch 'Rush Hour 2' and not get bored. We don't have the luxury of air conditioning or anything like that......Well... that was until a few days ago....

On the Palace grounds there are British, Norwegians, and Canadians a few Dutch and now we have been graced by the Americans.

Note all the fans around the TV trying to keep you cool in the communal room of the house. This was the only room where you would sit indoors.

When the Americans do something they don't piss about. Whilst we are sleeping on the roof and showering by pouring a bottle over our head, they detailed about a dozen squaddies to work from the Palace. Two weeks before they are due to turn up a couple of Graders go out and level a football pitch sized piece of waste ground. Then come along the lorries with their portacabin style toilets, ablutions and showers as complete units ready to be lifted into place, and finally, to top it off, more lorries turn up with accommodation blocks on them, again, ready to be ground set as complete units. For a few days chogies are busy plumbing it all in and making it operational.

If that wasn't enough a couple of thousand paving slabs finish the whole area off into a small American haven which looks amazing against the back drop of crap that we put up with. Peering through one of the windows I notice that in each of the bedrooms there is a bed with a cupboard and an armchair, each with its own air conditioning unit. An aircon unit each, now that's taking the piss a bit I think, especially considering that we don't have one between thirty.

So with that in mind, yesterday when I was walking back from the ops room I chose to walk through this new area, just to be nosey I guess. It was there that I saw them, some brand new, still boxed air conditioning units still waiting to be fitted all shiny and new, and... in the words of Martin Luther King,

*"I had a dream!!!!"*

I talked with some of the others when I got back to the house and then the plan was hatched. Like the Italian Job, each man knew his own job; each man knew every one else's job, what to do if someone were to come... and finally a cover story if we got caught. This was an important mission. Under the cover of darkness, we set off.

Two were in the LandRover and two of us were on foot as a look out. With the lights set to convoy on the Rover, it swung into position. One man jumped out of the Rover whilst the other helped with the goods. Not a word was said, each man executed the plan to perfection. Once it was loaded, the signal was given and the LandRover returned to the house. We all walked in separate directions finally meeting back at the house some time later.

The day had come...the day we all dreamed of since arriving!!

"WE HAVE AIRCONDITIONING"

We had just brought ourselves into the 1980's.

**GOD BLESS AMERICA!!!!**

Even Bobby the scouser would have been proud at this achievement. With the goods safely stashed in the house, we let a few days pass before letting the puppy out of her box and finally positioned it in the communal TV room. Nervous excitement was in the air as the power switch was flicked... she gave a noise not familiar to anyone as it began to bellow ice-cold air into the heat filled room, cheers went up from all when...only after a few seconds, all went quiet as the power failed. This time not with a power cut as we expected, but the simple electric fuse box in the house just couldn't cope with modern American technology. Someone immediately got on the mobile phone and cashed in a favour from one of the electrician's onsite and, before the day was out, we were cool. Now when we watch "Rush Hour 2" we are not sweating our nuts off, but it's still just as boring.

The boredom was broken on Monday of this week when we did a recce on a series of old port buildings adjacent to the river. On the Combat Support Boats (CSB's) were eight of us in total. The mission was to recce and take photographs of the disused buildings for habitation by the CF to use as a possible riverside base with all its obvious waterfront advantages.

On the CSB's, we were all tooled up in the usual manner, body armour etc.. It would take me a long time to get bored of travelling on these bad boys of the water. Moving north up river we yet again passed Saddam's Yacht. This time better prepared and being the tourist that I am I asked if we could go a little closer for photos etc. As we travelled around it, I wondered what it looked like back in the days when it was in all its glory. I have had an email from Craig, one of my pals who was mobilised on Op Telic , (the first wave of mobilisation), and he mentioned that he had been on it when it was afloat. I later found out that it finally keeled over onto its side on the 12th June 2003. It's around eighty metres in length and white, ignoring the great black holes caused by the bombs. The interesting thing now, is that it hasn't taken long for the looters to get to work on it with teams of chogies armed with blow torch cutting equipment, cutting the steel away in panels, (I told you these guys were good).

As well as the looters there are people swimming and using it as a diving board. Even here, as you pass on the CSB's the kids shout, "Mister Mister, Water Water", when you don't throw them anything they then shout the other bit of English they know "F**k Off Mister"

As the CSB's travelled further north passing all of the half sunken rusted ships, we moved closer to our target building. Using recent aerial photographs as maps, we found the best landing place. This happened to be a large port side industrial building with an internal docking area. It was a bit eerie at first moving into the building as the last time CF were around these parts, it was with the EOD who had swept through immobilising the surface to surface missiles that were still present in the buildings.

We pulled into the building directly from the river using the channel cut away to allow boats to enter the building. On each side above us were pilings that were sunk into the ground to form a channel, we all prepared to move out. Leaving the boat we took it in turns to clamber up the ladder made out of angle iron climbing up around eight feet to reach floor level. Each man was wearing his Personal Remote Radio (PRR), basically a small radio with headset and microphone positioned in front of your mouth Captain Scarlet style. We moved in pairs to do the Recce staying in constant contact with each other as we split up and went our separate ways. I set off with Jerome through the first of the buildings. My job was just to photograph every building inside and out, with Jerome recording what I shouted out with what and where they were on the map, giving a brief description what it was and the variety of angles shown of the same building, all so that a report could be formulated from our findings. It was as if time had stood still with this place. Imagine going back to a deserted industrial machining factory ten years after it was left half way through what ever it was doing, the only people visiting it were looters who took what they found valuable but left other things like documentation files and engineering drawings. There was even a plastic chair but I fought the temptation...after all, I already had one. Workbenches were strewn everywhere and bits of marine engines lay around, doors were missing leaving only the frames. Most of the buildings had already had the tin sheeting removed from the roof;

Would you buy a used forklift from this man?

basically all that was left was the stuff the looters did not want. The funny thing was though about this place, it had a load of machinery made in the UK. I had to smile when I saw the Overhead crane, made in Loughborough by Morris Cranes, one of my old forklift truck customers from a few years earlier. Forklift selling is a million miles away from this place. The buildings were all part of one original factory but in units varying in size from a few hundred square feet to massive hangar style buildings. Few were intact and even fewer had the corrugated roof, all had no doubt been squirreled away to make a shack somewhere else in Basra. As we walked around there was an old man and what looked like his grandson following us everywhere. Starting off looking on from afar, they eventually gained the confidence to come up close.

*"Hello mister"* shouted the child with a great smile on his face,
*"Hello"* I replied as he looked to his granddad for approval. His granddad gave an arm wave and spoke in Arabic with something that would have meant it's OK, carry on. He stood along side me looking up with a massive smile as he put his hand out to shake mine.

*"My name is Woody, What is your name?"* I said using the standard hand on the chest hand signal that crosses most language barriers.

*"Ali"* he replied. I looked down to see that Ali did not have any shoes on and his feet were all dried out in the searing heat and dust. He continually moved from heel to toe on each foot so as not to burn his feet

on the melting tarmac. This was something that he has obviously spent years doing as it came so naturally to him. His trousers were far too big for him and were held up with what looked like a thin strip of cloth torn from a chequered tablecloth. His T-shirt was dirty with a few weeks worth of grime; it had a small motif of a cartoon character on his chest. He appeared to be happy, but no one knows what he has seen and experienced in his little life.

I made some more hand signals to find out how old he was, he held up eight little fingers, the same age as Alex, my son. His granddad watched on as we carried on communicating, I couldn't help to draw a comparison between the short life that Alex has had compared to that of Ali. I gave him a small bottle of water and he was thrilled.

*"Hello please Mister"* he said as he walked back to his

Taken just as we had climbed the steps into the building from the boat clearly showing the large crane overhead. Note all the panels missing from the walls and the roof

granddad smiling. As Jerome and I made our way to the next building, he stood in the distance waving at us. To me it was just a bottle of water; to Ali it was probably the first fresh cold water he had drunk for a long time. Maybe it's something that Ali will remember for a long time... I hope so... I will.

We had been gone for about an hour and a half and all was going well with the recce when we heard two gunshots coming at us from just the other side of the ten feet high perimeter wall. All of a sudden this became real, a bit, 'too real' for my liking. Max was the first to hit the radios with
*"Was that you?"*
*"no"... "no"... "no"* as the answers came in from the three pairs out there.
*"Then who the f\*\*k was it then"* Max said
*"OK lads, eyes peeled, move it out"*
I thought, *"That's exactly what I was thinking, lets f\*\*k off, we've got loads of pictures so lets not push our luck any more!"*

The recce quickly turned into a patrol, as we made ready cocking our weapons. We all took cover by the nearest building. We began to make our way back to the CSB's patrolling aggressively. Now, for the last eleven years I have been on exercises where you patrol aggressively, (Walk with your weapon in the aim position showing that you mean business) however, whenever I have done it in the past the greatest threat that you had to worry about was whether you trod in dog shit, as Mrs Muggins walks her poodle past you on the training area as she calls out *"Good Morning"* and then goes on her way with little Fifi trotting along merrily without a care in the world. This was a bit different. On the training area when you are knackered you tend not to experience fear as it's not real, blank rounds and a bit of cam cream try to pep it up a bit, but the fact remains, it's training and the day will end. You have learned a bit about what it may be like but you won't get killed, and if you are hot and knackered, you stop and have a drink. Well here it was just over fifty degrees, plus, my body armour was causing my core body temperature to soar, my helmet was causing sweat to drip into my eyes and sting, my arms were aching but for a split second only, all of that was forgotten, my mind became occupied with more pressing matters. We all made our way back to the CSB's. We had done enough to form a report and we were not about to start looking out for the chogie with the AK47 attempting to make our acquaintance. Our job was done for today.

We got back onto the boats and quickly moved out.

Jerome and me in the port during the recce

What a great feeling to get the body armour and helmet off and feel the breeze against your soaking wet sweaty shirt as we moved back down river at speed back to the Palace. The only time we needed to put the helmets back on is when we travel under the old pontoon bridges with their low head room, the Iraqi kids seem to take great pleasure in throwing rocks as you travel underneath. Having pulled up into the small jetty within the palace, we then made our way across the grounds into the cookhouse in the Palace for our lamb dinner and ice-cream for pudding having completed just another day at work, for some it was all taken in their stride, as for me, I found it all interesting but not something I would want to do every day.

More to come...

Returning to the CSB after the recce of the port

Jerome looking across to the Palace Gates from the river

## OUR THOUGHTS GO OUT TO THEM

24th August 2003

By now you will all probably be aware of the attacks yesterday morning on the RMP vehicles in the centre of Basra. They were based here at the palace and travelling on a routine journey. My driving detail had just returned back from Basra International Airport travelling through the streets of Basra as we would do every day and finally back to the palace, returning at 8.20am. We had been in the ops room only some fifteen minutes when the news came in about the attack that had just happened at Red 17 at 8.30am, only ten minutes ago.

When I looked at the map I realised that we had just

travelled along that road passing the exact place, Red 17. I stood for a moment and thought about what could have been, and it proves the point that this is still a lottery when it comes to being in the right place or the wrong place at any given time. They were in the same style vehicles with the same number of people with only ten minutes separating them and us.

All the routes around the city have routes marked onto a spot map, a bit like a simplified version of the London Underground. This way you can easily quick reference routes and places when passing or receiving messages about specific locations.

The mood around the palace became very sombre and yet angry at why and how could this happen. No details were made official on the casualties but immediately a news and media block is placed, you know it's not good news. Out of respect for the families no names are released until the immediate relatives have been contacted, this prevents someone finding out about their loved one on the evening news. All mobile phone calls are barred and the Internet facility is immediately removed. This also makes it difficult to contact your own family to simply say, *"I'm OK"*. I spent almost twenty-four hours before I managed to get a message to Kerry to tell her that the TA Corporal based at the Palace in Basra, who had been killed was not I, but it also brought it home that someone had received the opposite of that news.

I realised later that all the attempts that I had made to contact Kerry were compounded by the fact that she had also missed some calls from an international telephone number. She began fearing the worst and began to panic as to the outcome. When she finally got the message that I was OK, she broke down.

New transport restrictions were immediately placed on all journeys (Confidentiality restricts me from telling you what they were). Then as the day passed all the people that I knew stopped moaning about how hot it was and other trivial details. We were all OK.

Earlier this morning we all went about our daily duties. (Out here it doesn't seem to matter what day it is i.e. Monday, Tuesday etc. it only matters what the date is, i.e. 24/8/2003. This is because every day is the same, you don't get weekends off and a Tuesday is the same as a Sunday), the sun always shines and nothing special happens to make one day different to the next. Almost like when you have two weeks off at Christmas and you know it's the day after boxing day, you know it's the 27th but you haven't got a clue if it's Tuesday or Saturday.

News got around that a Sunday remembrance service would be carried out later today for the RMP's killed in yesterday's attacks.

At 1600hrs soldiers gathered under the large balcony of the Palace on the Waters edge, shaded from the sun but overlooking the Shatt Al Arab river. Over a short period around two hundred soldiers gathered and formed up in a semi-circular shape, all stood looking out onto the river with the Padre as the focal point. All the RMP's along with the Military Police from the Ceczk Republic were to the front, with everyone else placed behind. All ranks were present from Privates to Brigadier.

A brief introduction was given by the Padre why we were here, naming the three soldiers individually and giving a short character description for each man. As I stood and listened to his words, the emotion and feelings got hammered home to me when the Padre said the words:

*"These men were Husbands, Fathers, Brothers, Sons and friends to a lot of people"*

I related very strongly to this as I mentally ticked them all off in my mind recognising that I was all of those things to my family and friends.

As the prayers continued I began thinking about my own family and how difficult it would be for them. I cannot begin to imagine what their family must be going through. Two buglers played the last post followed by a minute's silence to reflect and remember. At the end of the minute's silence a bagpipe player began to play whilst stood at the back of the congregation, no one turned around to look as he played, they only listened. The powerful sound of the pipes echoed underneath the balcony as we all stood silent. As he played, he began to walk away from where we were all standing, heading off along the riverside pathway. The sound of bagpipes always makes the hairs on the back of your neck stand up, but here, this was compounded by the occasion that this was real. It was difficult knowing that; we were here to remember people that were with us just over twenty-four hours ago. It then became more poignant as the sound of the pipes became distant; it felt as if their sprits were drifting away with the bagpipes.

By the time he had finished playing, he was a few hundred metres away in the distance with the pipes now very feint as he played his final notes. A silence fell over the gathered troops. The Padre summed up naming the wives and children of the three soldiers, asking for our thoughts to go out to them. I stood, along with over two-hundred other soldiers and fought back tears, knowing that it could have been any one of us stood there at that time. It was all very real; it's not like watching it on TV because you can turn the TV over... off... or simply walk away.

Here we are all immersed in it every day and cannot walk away. At the end of the service, the RMP's were the first to lead off in file, here there was no shame in crying, and they were friends of all three of these men. Each tried to comfort the next, most, simply asking "WHY?".
The area was then left for the RMP's to remember as the rest of the people went back to their jobs around the Palace grounds. I walked away wiping my eyes underneath my sunglasses; thinking, "there but for the grace of god!!!"

Earlier today, I drove past the place where yesterday's incident took place, it's a dual carriageway with a large disused water fountain in the central reservation where children use it to play and swim. Today as always, it was full of children playing.

Here life has to go on, but life will never be the same for the families of those three men.

My thoughts go out to them all.

More to come...

## IT'S ONLY A BRIDGE

### 29th August 2003

The last few days have passed pretty much the same as the rest. The milestone for me is the fifty-day mark. That's fifty days in theatre not fifty days since I left home, that adds another twenty-one days onto that figure. It also marks the halfway point for the tour. I guess you could say I am on the home stretch of the tour, or the back nine for all you golfers out there. My personal diary is becoming more mundane as time goes by with notes to myself such as, *"hand washed my sleeping bag earlier today, having dragged it out of the bucket weighing a tonne, threw it on a washing line and watched it dry completely in twenty minutes"*

---

During most of my correspondence I have knocked Iraq and what it looks like following the wrath of war, and let's face it, most of it deserving. All of the streets in Basra look the same. Nothing is finished and what is finished, was finished in the 1970's and has been falling to bits with thirty years of war to show as its scars. Basra was once a place that was thriving and where the people were allowed freedom, you can tell that from the faded grandeur that is still there. There is a large children's playground on the entrance into the Palace (outside the main gates) It has large climbing frames, huge boat swings and slides over twenty feet tall, there are picnic tables and fountains, large cartoon style animal structures, palm trees, a swimming pool that lies dormant and empty... This place once housed a lot of happiness and fun for children... now, it lies in tatters. The entire framework is rusting, the colours have all faded and is locked with barbed wire across the corroded gates. Across town there is a similar thing on the way to the old Naval Academy. It's an old zoo. The gates are there, the place is locked and it displays the same former qualities as the playground, now all over grown with once bright colours fading. It does make you think what happened to all the animals. The Iraqi's are not a great animal loving nation.

There is an alarming site that I pass every day when driving to the airport on the Motorway.

On the side of the motorway on what we would consider to be the hard shoulder, there are two rotting corpses of two adult sized camels. It's too hot for them to be covered in flies and there are no mosquitoes at this time of year, so... they are simply drying out in the sun. They are about fifteen feet apart and laying on what would have been their legs. They must have been tethered to the hard shoulder railings and left; they then could have sat down after a long while and then gave up waiting. It makes me wonder what happened to the camels, were they shot, who tied them up and why, who knows?... who cares?

In the back ground behind them there are five or six burned out tanks with their guns pointing in the same direction, out across the desert to defend Basra. Then beyond that there are burning oil fields.
This scene depicts a lot about Iraq in one shot.
As I have said before, the Iraqis are not a nation of animal lovers.

There are three things you would not want to be in Iraq.

1. A Donkey.
2 A Dog,
3. A Woman.

The streets are filled with packs of stray dogs, foraging and fighting for whatever they can scavenge from the rubbish that lies around.

The donkeys have a shit time. They all seem to have weeping open sores from being constantly whipped in the same place. As you drive past them in heavy traffic you can see the sun glistening on the open flesh on their back. They do the best they can whilst pulling a heavy weight on a cart, a weight that we would normally move on a lorry.

---

The women, on the other hand, always seem to be walking, miles from nowhere in the searing heat with oversized parcels on their heads whilst covered from head to toe in black, you rarely see an Iraqi woman smiling, and seeing what they have to deal with on a daily basis, would you want to smile?

There are things that have made me smile though. Every day from around 3.00pm onwards there are a masses of cars being valeted, anywhere there is water, be it a river or a puddle, there will be crowds of people washing cars. All you need to set up your own little enterprising business is a vegetable oil tin, a sponge and a puddle. These small businesses line the roads. These are the very cars that are absolutely beaten to bits and most worthy of the UK scrap yards. Over here they are their life and they take such pride in them. They are all very car proud. You will never see a dusty or dirty Iraqi car, every panel will be battered, it may have no head lights or even no windscreen, but it will not be dirty, especially the taxis, these drivers take great pride in their cars. They are the ones with orange panels on each wing front and rear and represent 75% of the cars on the roads.

That's what life is like in the city, but two days ago I saw another side to Iraq when I did a driving detail with a bit of a difference. The difference being that we ventured out of Basra and into the sticks a bit more, heading south down the river. I have driven north of Basra on many occasions but that takes you more into the flat faceless dusty desert, same colour, and same boring views. This was different; the fresh water rivers gave a welcome splash of colour.

We drove for about an hour in two open top LandRovers, two people in the front and each with a person sticking out the top as 360-degree gun cover. This is a result of the savage attacks last week.

We followed a main supply route parallel with the river, in the main it was very similar to the areas around Basra, but more sparsely populated. As we travelled we passed through two PVCP's (Permanent Vehicle Check Points) These are manned by Iraqi Police and stop any vehicles they wish, searching them looking for guns, explosives, stolen goods, or anything suspicious.

When you pass through these places, the police are always pleased to see you and will always wave you on through ahead of the other traffic. After the PVCP's we then made a couple of turns that brought us running closer to the river. This is where I noticed a big difference. The city I have described and would be a bit of a misery to live there, as I am sure you will appreciate. This area was different. On both sides of the narrow road were palm trees, not just a couple but great woods of them. Dotted in the palm trees were houses, all very spaced out, and, dare I say it, but it looked a nice place. The ground was very well irrigated with small channels cut in, allowing the water to feed life into the land. This place was green.... there's nothing green in Iraq, or so I thought. As we drove along the narrow roads, I also noticed another big difference, the children would run and shout with happiness as you pass, all waving in the hope that you would see them and wave back, not because they were after something. This we all did with pleasure. The other difference was the adults did the same, but with less energy...but the gratitude behind the wave was equally as strong.

In the city the kids are waving with a hidden agenda as they beg for water and sweets. The city kids are very street wise and turn on you the second they realise they will not get water from you, many will have had a lifetime of begging, even kids as old as ten will have never known any other way of life other than war, repression and begging. This was different.

This was their equivalent of the countryside. As we drove through it reminded me a bit (and I mean only a bit) of Centre Parcs with little houses hidden and dotted in amongst the trees. The big difference was that these kids were not wearing white shell suits and gold trainers!!

We approached a small village that was bustling with people as we crawled our way along the main street. I felt very relaxed and happy as we drove down that street. Everyone waved, some placing their hands to their heart as if to say a heart felt thanks for what the CF had done in the last few months and what we're still doing today. I turned to my mate Bov who was sat next to me driving the LandRover and we agreed that this made it all worthwhile. We were relaxed, we didn't feel threatened in the way you do as you drive through some of the areas in the city.... and, they were happy to see us. Along from the main street were small businesses with their children helping them on the stall for whatever they were selling? There was a melon stall with more melons than I have ever seen in one place. There was a man and his son weaving grass matting and the smell reminded me of a hayloft as we drove past. There was a small garage with a kid in a small pair of overalls just like his dads as they stood out the front working on someone's car.

That brought a smile to my face as it reminded me of when I was younger helping my Dad do the same. If there were a place where you would have to live in Iraq, this probably would be it.... And if nothing else...at least you would be guaranteed the weather!

As we passed the main street we took another right turn over a bridge that must have been there a fair few years, it was part metal and part wooden, it had been repaired many times over, it bore a Royal Engineers plaque on it stating the name and date of when it had been last repaired. Below that in the small river, kids played diving from a tiny boat.

My mate Bov keeping the children entertained. Every time you stop, children come to the window begging.

As they saw us they shouted *"Hello Mister"* and then all performed their dives for us from the boat...showing off. One even did a somersault as his grand finale to top what his mates had just performed, these kids seemed happy. It was great to see having seen so many kids suffering in the past.

We then entered what I can only describe as being the 'Posh End' of town. These people had got new grass matted fences around their plots, the kids were better dressed than in the city, the little girls had pretty little flowered dresses on and all had the smiles to match. It made me think that if the little girls are all so pretty, at what point in their life do they turn into the old women that we were familiar with in the cities. All having harsh sun scorched skin plus a life of dealing with survival on a daily basis probably gives them very little to smile about. Hopefully this will change in the future.

A fair few of the houses in this area had the type of minibus you expect to see in a Hollywood film about Colombian drug barons. Very old Chevrolet vans with wooden framework around the back and great bulbous style bonnets, probably late 1950's or early 1960's, they looked a bit like a Morris Minor Traveller but the size of a Transit van.

This area was reminiscent of a plantation, and the whole place had a very relaxed atmosphere. Out here they would have been under Saddam's rule but they also had their own community, something that I couldn't see happening in a big city. With Saddam out of the way their small community was allowed to flourish.

---

Another reason for their happiness in seeing the CF in the area was soon apparent, when we approached the task area where the Norwegian Army (Engineers) were working. The bridge spanned about a fifteen-metre gap and a small slow flowing river of fresh water meandered below.

It had been damaged in the first Gulf war in 1990 and had cut the area in two. The Norwegians have stripped out the old bridge and were repairing it with a new Bailey type bridge. As we pulled up the kids were running to greet us as we looked at the site with the old bridge now stripped out on the banks.
The new bridge will be in place within two weeks. The first time for over thirteen years, this small community will be brought back together. It's only a bridge to us, but to them it opens the whole area back up again and gives them back what they once had.

As we left, both the kids and the adults were waving, something that doesn't happen in the city, but as I said, this place was different. Again it's small things like this, that makes it all worthwhile.

As we retraced our steps through the same roads we passed through earlier. I thought to myself.
*"I enjoyed today!"*

More to come...

# ROUTINE

## 30th August 2003

There is no pattern to this, I just try and cover things that people may find interesting, and as this has been a low news day, I thought I would cover the mundane elements of the tour.

I will cover my usual routine on an *'Ops Room'* Day. Waking to the usual cries from the Mosques gets me out of bed, and following a shower, I get my uniform on and make my way across three-hundred metres of what used to be front garden to get some breakfast. Eating a full English every day with sweat dripping from your nose can sometimes be a little hard to bear so I tend to go for the cold option of fruit and cereals.

---

Leaving the cookhouse I cross one of the many bridges and head to the main palace, which is about a further four hundred metres. Outside the main palace there are always a collection of vehicles waiting to take someone, somewhere. The drivers sitting round waiting 'the call'.

My first job is to get a handover from the person who is just finishing his shift on the Engineers Ops desk. The hand over covers everything that happened in the night, each call that was made and what actions still need to be followed up. I cover two radios, a landline telephone and a couple of mobile phones. Each call has to be logged and messages passed on. Put simply, I am a receptionist.

Sitting around the same desk are officers and other people that outrank me three times over, however as time has gone on in this environment, although I am the lowly Corporal, I have started to find my feet and confidence applying what I do well as a civilian both customer facing and in a sales office. In short I talk to people and make things happen. This is no different, only here, at the end of every sentence I must remember to keep saying *"sir"*.

During the day to relieve the boredom one of the officers once suggested that we all play a game called 'Spoof'. This consists of being issued three Iraqi coins that are your spoof coins. You then hide a number of coins in a clenched fist in the air and take turns to guess at the total number of coins being held by everyone. The winner does NOT have to make the Tea. The game starts again until only one person remains. He or she then makes the tea or coffee for everyone that played the game.

––––––––

I took great pleasure in saying the words *"Coffee, white with one please"* to a Major who then gets to his feet and brings me my drink. Applying a bit of civilian common sense, I made a cardboard plastic cup holder with each persons name next to a cup hole detailing what that person drinks and how they take it. I kept it safe in the bottom drawer and proudly produced it whenever I lost and it was my turn to make the drinks. *"Woody... it's obvious that you're a civvy because you apply common sense too often"* said one officer when I carried back a round of drinks in one hand.

Also to pass the time someone would bring in some sweets that they had received in their parcels from home and share them around. One of the great pleasures here is getting a parcel from home and not knowing what could be inside, giving a short burst of excitement as you tear it open with others staring over your shoulder joining in the moment with a hope that

Here is a parcel from my mother, a good choice, peanuts, a bit of reading material, a bluey, some sweets and a bit of whisky.

they will get a bit of what you have received. Only here will you see anticipation in the face of a Major in the British Army hoping that he will get one of your wine gums.

The day drags but it's very interesting to see what is going on around the whole of the Basra area as the reports come in. The working day finishes around 1730hrs, I then take the ten minute walk from the main palace along the river and across one of the many ornate hump back bridges crossing a water inlet from the main river, filling one of the two large lakes. When I say hump back bridge I really mean hump back, i.e. every time you cross it in a LandRover your stomach hits the back of your head. The walk along the river is probably one of the best things about this place; the river is about 250m wide and flowing from left to

The hump back bridge in the palace where I crossed each day, the river is to the right.

165

right. The palaces here are connected by a promenade style walkway matching the light sandstone used for all the palace buildings. This stretches along the entire length of the palace grounds with one of the main gates also sitting on the banks of the river. It's an awesome sight from the river, to approach from the north and pass the buildings.

I then generally go into one of the Internet booths to see if they are working and pick up my emails and write some more of the story. A private company who supply telephone and Internet facilities provides the welfare facilities, however their performance of late has left a bit to be desired. One portacabin houses eight telephones. That's eight telephones between around four hundred troops. They are all satellite phones with the mother of all dishes placed at the end of the building. These telephones have been down now for just over three weeks, they say awaiting parts.

How come the parcels of Scottish Pure Malt cough medicine that my wife sends me only take five days to arrive and yet we have been waiting three weeks to phone home because they can't get hold of the jiggle pin or whatever it is that's missing from their system.

As I said, Disgraceful!!!

The internet that is provided is very useful but very slow and temperamental, it can take up to ten minutes to log-on resulting in your twenty minutes being swallowed up very quickly and not much time to read and send emails. The buildings consist of three small booths each housing five terminals. Each booth has one small air conditioning unit. If the computers are working then the aircon generally is not and vice-versa. It's not uncommon to look along the row of terminals and see four other people all with sweat dripping from them as they type. All in all, pretty poor, but better than not having them at all.

So from the Internet, if it's working I check my emails and then go for scoff at 1800hrs.

'Scoff' ... That's one of the words that enters your vocabulary when you arrive in theatre, obviously it means eat. There are plenty of new words that I have picked up since being out here.

For e.g. "Dhobi" and "Hanging out yer arse"

Dhobi, means doing your clothes washing, it comes from an Indian word.... where the dhobi whalla's wash and iron your clothes professionally by hand in a dhobi village where generations of the same family work using very primitive methods but with startling results.

I have heard a few of the lads using another great saying when they are a bit pissed off.

*"It's all cake and arse, but without the cake"*
I haven't got a clue what it means but it just sounds great.

*"Hanging out yer arse"* however is generally used to describe how hot and tired you are. Now I have checked on a number of occasions when I have been both hot and tired and never has there been anything other than the usual in the area of my tradesman's entrance to justify the description. Still, I never

question why, I just insert the new words into my every day life in a bid to simply blend in.
Use the lingo and *'hey presto'*, you're a squaddie.

After scoff I then take the five-minute walk back to the house. The walk takes me across what now looks like wasteland but was once a grassed area with palm trees on it and an irrigation system feeding life into what would have been well manicured gardens tended by gardeners turning this garden into a flourish of green in an otherwise colourless environment...all whilst working under very strict life or death guidelines no doubt. In its day it must have looked stunning but at what cost, be that financial or human. The irrigation system is probably the size of three football pitches, obviously much needed in the heat, and without it the area would have only taken a matter of a few days to become completely arid once more as it is today. From the wasteland I go past the tank park with different types of small recce tanks and APC's (Armoured Personnel Carriers) used by the infantry boys from the QLR (Queens Lancashire Regiment).
These tanks are parked on what would normally be the central reservation of a small dual carriageway. Passing that you then enter what is known as Brookside Close. So called, because it's a small cul-de-sac of seven houses, three on one side, four on the other. It's similar to any other cul-de-sac in suburbia, accept all the houses have the same company car here, the LandRover in a nice shade of Tuscan Beige. As I get home there will always be people sitting out the front on the old settee with shorts and flip-flops. A quick grunt of "Hiya" normally gets thrown back and forth then I enter the house to my room at the back.

The room is the same as the rest of the house with marble floors and cream coloured faceless brick. I share the room with two other people, One Sapper and a Lance Corporal. The room is just a place to store your kit and get changed etc..

My cupboards are made of two boxes of bottled water, still full, as they are to give strength to the base of the structure. On top of that I have four empty boxes lain on their sides with the tops open so as to form four internal shelves for my tee shirts and clean uniform. On top of them I have a box with separate compartments for my socks, underwear and miscellaneous stuff like Dogtags, ID card, pens etc, and as before, all made from empty bottled water boxes. It pays to be organised, and you are never short of time to get organised, so out here there is no excuse

Here I sit with some of the other engineers assuming the usual position outside the house. Next to me on the settee is Eddie, next to him with the bottle is Sprucey. I'm not sure of the name of the guy on the right but he turned himself into a press-up machine doing over 1000 press-ups every day. He said; "I'm going home with muscles and a suntan"... it worked!

for being sloppy.

Above that on the wall there are a large selection photos of Kerry, the children, and parents. These help to give me a reality check. With each parcel that arrives from my wife, I get another selection of photos from sometime in our life, each time giving me another injection of family memories. If you have photos on the wall at home, you never stop and stare at them; you just walk past and carry on going about your business. Here it's different, I find myself staring at them for ages and reliving the moment when the picture was taken. It reminds me that I have a life outside of this shit hole. I even have things to smell, my wife has sent me a small bottle of the perfume that she wears, it's a smell that is definitely worth a thousand words as there is no finer smell on this earth

My cardboard bedroom furniture keeping my kit organised. All my photos are just above on the wall.

than the smell of my wife. Smell is such a wonderful way to spark off the memories. Have you ever tried smelling suntan lotion whilst looking at your summer holiday photos and it's the middle of winter; try it you will see what I mean!!!

In front of my box structure cupboard I have a lockable tin footlocker box that I signed for at Shaibah. This is where I keep my weapon and ammunition, you are responsible for your own weapon and it has to go everywhere I do. Running along side that I have a cot bed, this is the same collapsible camp bed that I once fought with the first night in Kuwait, now though I use it only to sit on, not sleep on. I tried to sleep on it once and nearly drowned in my own sweat. Under my bed I have what every kid dreams of........... A shoebox full of goodies like wine gums, jelly beans, biscuits, pork scratchings and a load of other stuff that is bad for me. I love to get back at the end of the day and open my box of goodies, never eating more than a couple of things because you never know when the next parcel will arrive so I just ration myself to the bare minimum.

First job is to get out of the desert gear and get my shorts and flip-flops on. I then have the choice, do I go into the TV room with our yanky aircon and sit through "Rush Hour 2" again or do I do my dhobi. I must admit the dhobi usually gets done because as soon as I get comfortable in the TV room the power normally goes and I end up sitting in the pitch dark with ten other blokes all afraid to move first. Doing my dhobi by torchlight is a bit of a pain in the arse so the dhobi normally gets done first.

---

It gets dark here around 2000hrs so that's normally it for the evening, no bar, no social club, no nothing! The highlight of the night is going for a shower!

That was until my first bottle of whisky made it through the postal system disguised in a bottle of Panda Pops hidden inside a tube of Pringles. Half of the Pringles had been removed and the pop bottle was covered in kitchen roll, on top of that were placed more Pringles onto which the foil seal was replaced and the plastic top secured. Ingenious. They were so well hidden that it was a couple of days before I felt like the Pringles and to my amazement, I found the whisky. Well-done Mother!! Totally against the rules but I wasn't about to get pissed, I was more interested in making it last as long as possible to savour it as I never knew when a top up was about to arrive.

I tend to go to bed around 2100hrs through boredom and because it takes me ages to get to sleep. A quick trip to the chemical toilet before hitting the sack, and I mean a quick trip. You definitely do not sit here reading the back of a shampoo bottle. It's in and out, normally all done with one breath.

Then it's up to the roof to get onto my bed, (not into as there are no need for quilts here), I now have a proper wooden bed with a proper mattress and a fitted sheet with matching a pillowcase covering my special brown patterned pillow to which I have become so attached. The bed and the mattress were 'borrowed' from another camp when on a driving detail there a few weeks back. As for the fitted sheet and pillowcases, I have my mother-in-law to thank for that. My first job before getting onto the bed is to strip the fitted sheet off and shake off the top layer of sand that has blown on throughout the day. I then apply the important part of my sleep system, two yellow earplugs to deaden the noise of gunfire, helicopters and the early morning mosques. I use a rolled up T-shirt to cover my eyes and mop the sweat. Months of trial and error have developed this complete system but it still takes ages to drop off with either gunfire or helicopters patrolling, but eventually you find yourself at 0400hrs the sun is coming up and you are woken by the wailing of the prayer callers from the all the mosques, you are knackered and ready to start another day, that is if I make it through the night without being called out, as my duty changes at midnight from ops room to escort commander.

More to come...

My wooden bed in the mosquito net with fitted sheet and sacred
pillow with a fantastic view across the lake at the Palace and onto
the river

## PORK SCRATCHINGS IN BASRA

7th September 2003

"The days seem to be dragging but the weeks are flying by", that's how someone described it here, and I think they are right.

Over the last few weeks the driving has become a bit scarier in one respect due to the incidents that are still happening. The big difference in safety comes from how the vehicles are prepared now. All the LandRover's have been stripped down to their shell with the hard top roof removed and the cab roof removed. This leaves just the roll bars. Onto this has been placed cages covering all sides, windows and roof. Above the drivers cab is placed a Hessian material to shade the driver and commander from the

sun. All vehicle moves now still need a minimum of
two vehicles but now each must have at least six
people with three in each vehicle. One driver, a
vehicle commander and top cover.

The guy who is top cover has the job of standing up in
the rear of the vehicle with his head and rifle either
pointing forward, if he's in the front vehicle or
backward in the rear vehicle. Some vehicle moves need
twin top cover both forwards and backwards on each
vehicle, it all depends on the current state in the city
at that time. The other key difference now is that if
you go out of camp now you are always made ready.
That means your weapon is cocked and ready to fire.
Only the safety catch needs to be removed before the
action starts.

It's difficult trying to keep both vehicles together when moving through the
traffic in the town.

The first time I did top cover was ten days ago when I was forward facing on the front vehicle. We had received intelligence to suggest that there were crowds gathering, but still we needed to get across town to get to the airport. As we left the palace, I couldn't help noticing that everyone is staring at you perched on the roof as you point your weapon back. Well that's the theory; in fact you are fighting to keep your balance as your vehicle screams through the traffic. Your job is to watch everyone and every vehicle in your arc of fire to spot people who could become a possible threat. The recent attacks to the RMP's were from a vehicle that pulled alongside and opened fire without them seeing the approach. Now it was different... We are now dealing with a different set of rules altogether.

The time was around 10am as we travelled through Basra along one of the main streets. From my position on top I could see a large crowd gathered about 400mts ahead. As we got to within 200mts I noticed three or four Iraqi police running towards us waving their arms frantically. By the time I had radioed to the driver on the PRR, we had just driven straight into a funeral of a local that was killed by the CF yesterday. To our left we had a two feet high concrete central reservation; to our right we had a series of large concrete flowerbeds. We were trapped. There were around seven hundred and fifty people running toward our vehicles all waving their arms, people coming at us from all directions. My driver put it into reverse but couldn't move backwards because our escort driver (the second vehicle of the two) had closed the gap between our vehicles just as a couple of coaches pulled up behind him. At this point my rifle was up in the aim and safety catch off. (I am not too proud to say I was shitting myself at this point) The escort driver began to shunt the two coaches behind him backwards to create enough room for him to do a three-point turn and us to follow. By this time many people were surrounding the vehicles all shouting and waving their arms trying to get to us. I could see the rage and passion in the eyes of the people around us. As they screamed and chanted I could see the spit of one man as he shouted at us. They wanted us dead, no matter by what means, they were in a frenzy and we were in the middle of it. The drivers found a gap in the central reservation just big enough to squeeze through to escape. As we drove down the wrong side of the road weaving through traffic there were still crowds of people coming out of side streets and shouting at us. My heart was leaping out of its skin as we headed back to the palace. That was a close one, maybe a bit too close for a forklift truck salesman.

As we got to the end of that Dual carriageway a police car had just pulled up and now stopped all traffic from going down that route. As we pulled back into the safety of the Palace grounds I got down from the vehicle and began to clear my weapon in the unloading point, it was then that I immediately felt ill and threw up. As I looked down, I couldn't tell if my trousers were wet through with sweat or because I pissed myself through fear. I have a feeling it was the latter but kept quiet about it, as it's not something you want to shout about to your mates. I was just happy to be alive.

Once back in the Ops room we shared our knowledge of the funeral, the crowds and the general threat, as they then rendered that area out of bounds sending a signal to that effect to all of the other squadrons so that no one else entered that area.

Later on in the week I was providing top cover for the escort vehicle and we were heading out along what is known as route *'Bone'* so called because it shakes every bone in your body. The route is around 12km long and is an off road desert track with the occasional piece of rough tarmac just to remind the driver that he is still somewhere on earth. Due to some big cheeses bad planning we had to travel along this route four times consecutively with yours truly hanging on to the roof all the way. Please imagine if you will, sitting in a tumble dryer on high setting, then you probably won't be far from the *'Route Bone'* experience. What else I experienced for the first time was being in the middle of the mini tornado called a *'dirt devil'*. Just as in the *'Wizard of Oz'* there is a large tube going up to the sky with a huge cloud of dust and litter swirling around. It was perfectly safe in every way but very spectacular to be in the middle of. I did exactly as Dorothy was instructed to do...I clicked my heels three times and said *"there's no place like home"*, and found I was still standing on the roof of a LandRover in the middle of the desert with a gun in my hand.

*"Oh Bollocks...worth a try I guess"*

Out here in the desert, it's not like you would imagine. When anyone says desert, you immediately imagine flowing hills of soft white sand and if you are old enough, you will probably conjure up memories of some dusky maiden with sultry eyes walking along the sand ridge wearing sandals whilst eating a Turkish Delight. All you get here is white dirt, dust and litter with the frequent waft of excrement and crude oil. Not quite the same romantic image really!.

I was on Top cover for over seven hours in total that day having set off at 1030hrs and returning just before 1800hrs. That is a long time to be in the sun with your helmet and body armour on. When I got down from the vehicle I took off my body armour and went into the Palace Ops room to check the vehicle back in again and that's when I almost passed out. I think it was the sudden change in temperature coupled with general heat exhaustion. To keep the body functioning you need to drink six to eight litres of water per day minimum depending on what activity you are doing,

The typical view when you are on 'Top Cover'

plus you need to take at least five salt sachets with every meal. This keeps your salt levels high enough, allowing your body to function. Dehydration drinks that provide the correct balance of salt in your blood stream can supplement this. The biggest water loss comes from wearing the body armour over the top of your clothing during the day. When it's on you can't feel the sweat at all, it's a bit like wearing a wet suit, and when you take it off you're completely soaked through. During this day I had taken on around six litres of water but no salt and that's what took its toll on my body.. It took me around three days to fully recover from that. Wearing your helmet and sand goggles also causes a great deal of discomfort during your working day. Thanks to Kerry for my plentiful supply of Pork Scratching to help get my salt levels back up. Surprisingly there are not many Butchers in Basra that sell Pork scratchings.

Here a child waits in the desert, bare foot, hoping to get thrown a bottle of water from passing troops as the temperature reaches almost sixty degrees.

I was glad to see the back of August, as it got hotter than July, if that was at all possible. It was reaching highs of fifty-eight degrees in the day and still in the mid forties at night. The chogies call August *'The Oven'* for the obvious reason. It slowly takes its toll on your body as I found out.

More to come...

---

## CPL WOODHALL PORN STAR

17th September 2003

I am now getting bored with the day-to-day grind of life out here with each day blending into the next. At least my routine rotates every two days not every day, as is the case with most other people. However, I also found myself, with little else to write about without repetition or covering stuff that has been done in the past. I am now trapped in this world of investigative journalism, for my growing readership of *'hundreds of people'* all yearning for more, each, I was told, trying to satisfy that 'mid morning coffee break' time with an email that provides a bit of escapism from their daily routine.

---

Having covered most subjects experienced, I spoke with the Boat Operators who go out at all hours on patrols along the river, and volunteered for a boat patrol in the early hours of the morning. As long as it didn't conflict with my normal duties, I would be in the clear. My reporting time for the patrol was 0430hrs in the Ops room at the Palace. I didn't know much of the patrol or what it involved; I just knew my reporting time and the kit required. I planned to get some sleep, as I would be up early. I managed to get my head down at around 2030hrs having finished my dhobi for the day. Earplugs in, towel across the face, head on the sacred pillow... it didn't take long for me to drift away. I was woken at 2200hrs with a driving detail taking place in the early hours. We were to collect the new Ops Officer from the airport at 0150hrs, I didn't want to mention my Boat Op to anyone... so having done a quick time appreciation in my head, worked it out that I could fit both in, but with no sleep...just.

We left the palace at 0100hrs. We loaded our weapons in the loading bay outside the house on the front garden. The loading bay is a four-post stillage filled with gravel and a couple of plastic water pipes sticking out to the top at an angle. This allows you to load and more importantly, unload your weapons safely in a controlled environment. An ND or, 'Negligent Discharge' is when a weapon has not been cleared correctly and a round is accidentally fired. This is a chargeable offence for the culprit costing as much as £1000 or worse, someone's life, from a careless round being shot accidentally.

With our weapons loaded and made ready, a quick comm's check on the PRR's and we were on our way out of the palace gates. Driving during the day is bad enough as there is a lot of traffic and plenty of unknowns, Driving at night is different...a lot different. As we left the gates we could here the gunfire in the distance echoing around. It's very difficult to pinpoint exactly which direction it's coming from and gunfire is common for any night. The tribal fighting usually takes place between many of the local political wings and petty criminals. The solution to most nighttime disagreements out here is normally delivered from an AK47.

Without trying to sound mellow dramatic, most times I drove out of the palace, I thought to myself, *"Is today my time to go"*. I would never get used to the feeling of standing at the exit to the Palace, staring into the darkness, listening to the gunfire and thinking, *"I cannot believe I am about to drive through that, I did it yesterday and was lucky, am I pushing my luck by doing it again tonight?"* I would always breathe a great sigh of relief as we returned through the palace gates hours later.

Working in the Ops room does that to you as you get to hear about every shotrep (Report of a shooting) and any other serious incident in the whole of the Basra Province. You begin to believe that almost everyone is being attacked outside the safety of the Palace walls.

A few weeks back, around 2200hrs, there was a large explosion about 100m outside the palace gates. The QRF (Quick Reaction Force) and EOD (Explosive

Ordnance Disposal) were dispatched to immediately check it out. We all speculated that it could be a suicide bomber or a previously placed car bomb that was detonated by a timer. It transpired that some chogie was getting a bit fed up with other chogies parking their cars and having a drinking session outside his house every night. He explained that if they did it again he would blow up their car. The next night they were back armed with the cans of cheap beer ready to enjoy another drinking session, so he addressed the issue with 10lbs of Semtex.

Tonight it was very quiet but still pitch black as you pick your way through the Basra streets on the way out to the airport. The route first takes you along the riverside gate of the palace with the river to your right and the disused playground to your left, after about 400m we take a left turn and out on to one of the main routes used. As you join the main road there is a three-feet wide hole in the middle of the road caused by either a small explosion or a directed bomb of some sort. You can see the steel wire supporting the road and then straight through onto the river below. The only thing warning of this hole for the motorist or pedestrian is a small vegetable oil tin placed directly to the front of the hole. The first part of the journey is very built up with buildings on both sides of the road, all the buildings are in a very poor state of repair, if not destroyed totally from air strikes. The traffic lights are there but not working, these are now manned during the day with newly trained Iraqi police all armed with a whistle where they have each proudly developed their own distinct warble to summon the traffic along. We then go through the centre of Basra, an area that has a series of shops and small businesses. I have been through this area at night on many occasions. The most spectacular time is between 2000hrs and midnight on a Saturday night. That's when this place comes alive. During the day the place is busy but only with traffic, few people venture out due to the heat. On a Saturday night it turns into a market place, a meeting place and an area for people to come out to shop and escape the intense and relentless daytime heat, even though at midnight it is still over 40 degrees in August.

This is a typical view from the window of a LandRover with another destroyed building from the conflict.

Max and I chatted as we drove through the market place, sat in almost stationary traffic taking over an hour to cover just a couple of miles. It's very intimidating moving so slowly in such a crowded area. You would be amazed at what people are selling, laying their wares on the side of the road. It reminded me of a car boot sale only not selling plastic tat. One guy had a pile of corrugated iron sheeting for sale all rusting and otherwise useless, probably from the building where we did the port recce. Another had a pile of nuts and bolts all randomly spread across the centre of the road. One guy was selling second hand carpet, you could see where it had been previously cut and fitted. As you drive through this environment you don't have speed on your side as a means of escape. You are stationary or at best crawling along at less than walking pace with the rest of the traffic. As people walk by, they all stare at you as you stare back with a smile... with your helmet and body armour, sitting in your LandRover dripping with sweat, as you point a friendly rifle back in their general direction. What they must be thinking, Allah only knows! I'm very uncomfortable in this environment as I worry what they are thinking as they stare at me. I want to hold up cards in Arabic saying *"I only want to help"*

Children are everywhere. It's not uncommon to see a child as young as five carrying a baby only a few months old, walking in and out of the traffic in the dark begging for water. As a father of three children I could never get used to this. As I said before, you must not give water out as you simply open the floodgates for beggars, and would probably get mobbed in the process, but as hard as it is, and

---

knowing that it is wrong, everyone still does it out of compassion.

The men around here fall into a few categories. Teenage boys dressed in football shirts, they stand in crowds shouting abuse at you in Arabic followed by group laughter. A chogie interpreter once told me that women are for babies and Men are for loving. It is not uncommon to see young men holding hands when stood in communal groups in the town.

It would be wrong for me to say that Iraq is full of homosexuals, clearly this is not the case, but the two cultures are completely different in every facet of life, with this being only one small area, men holding hands here is the norm. To quote an equally unusual trait I would bring to your attention how we find it totally acceptable for a woman to sit topless on a beach when on holiday, when Arabic men would not consider this as acceptable and almost impossible to accept as the norm. We are simply different... nothing more.

You then have the thirty something men who dress smartly and are clean-shaven, wearing shirt and trousers, walking with a purpose. Finally you have the fifty plus men who all wear traditional dish-dash and shemagh, sporting long beards and a thousand facial lines telling of their long struggle. If anyone ever wanted convincing of the damage that too much sun does to the skin, have a look at these guys.

We carried on our route through Basra across six or seven traffic islands and out toward the Naval

Academy. This area is used for the payment of the Iraqi Army and Police. When this British Army run operation first began a few months back it was total mayhem with thousands of men turning up, all claiming to be ex Police, Navy or Iraqi Army (Not Saddam's Republican Guard), now the filtering has taken place it runs very smoothly processing and paying these people every other Thursday.

Taking a left turn away from the river, you move along a dual carriageway with the buildings now set way back from the road. Towards the top of this road is one of the two petrol stations in the area. Along side the petrol station is where fuel is decanted into smaller containers for further distribution by donkey or chogie bike. The floor is covered in thick black oil slurry and the whole area has a foul crude oil stench twenty-four hours per day. During daylight hours there are always a group of chogies with donkeys and carts bartering for the fuel. It always amazes me when, during the day I see people standing in this black oil slurry... barefoot.

As we pass now at 0100hrs... the stench is still heavy in the air with of a mixture of crude oil, petrol and diesel oil all mixed as the warm air hits my face as we drive by. That road takes us along to a main crossroads where we take a right turn out of town. The road is now the equivalent of three lanes wide for each carriageway. I say equivalent as there are no white lines marking the lanes on the road, it just remains a 'free for all' when driving. There are no streetlights on this stretch of road so you need to be alert when driving after dark, as many of the vehicles have no headlights, stray dogs become the king of the streets hunting in packs for what ever they can get. Last week I passed here to see that a horse had died and was simply left on the side of the road, less than twenty-four hours later all that remained was a skeleton with more than fifty dogs filling the area, scavenging what was left of the carcass.

We eventually move out onto the motorway, the driving here can be a little less stressful because we are now out of the town with its heavy population where the one off... 'Have a go' hero to takes his pot shot from a balcony... here we are now in an area where if anything is going to happen it's usually well planned and well executed with a remote device that can be triggered from five hundred metres away. The road takes us over a relatively new bridge that has had one of its two large bridges completed. It was originally planned for this great bridge to have a separate bridge for each directional lane, however, only one ever got completed... so you have to travel across rough ground to come in the opposite direction and all use the same bridge.

We move quickly onto the Airport located about 15km out of Basra. When we get to the airport we have about a one-hour wait before the officer comes out to meet us. We give him his body armour and helmet and following a quick comms check, we move out back to the palace. On the way back I sit and chat with him as I drive through the streets. His visit here is his first, and although he is a Captain and probably has a wealth of experience in a vast amount of situations, here though, he is the new kid and I am the one with the vast array of new found experiences to share and feel quite pleased that I can answer his questions and offer useless advise that will make his life a little easier during his stay.

We get back at just after 0330hrs. I decide not to go to bed, as I needed to be in the Ops room for the Boat patrol in less than an hour. I chose to go straight to the Ops room in the palace to wait there. The main hall of the palace is a cathedral of a place during the day when it is filled with people all forming the various cells that make up the brigade machine with this being its beating heart, but at night, each cell will have one person who drew the short straw, manning the cells as a phone or radio watch during the wee small hours. At each desk sits someone filling in the time in their own special chosen way, a word search, a crossword, the latest book borrowed from the welfare building, last weeks newspaper, writing a bluey to their loved one or just staring at the ornate ceiling in wonderment thinking what used to go on in this place less than a few months ago, all in all, it's a totally different atmosphere than during the day.

Running a few minutes late, the Boat Ops turn up to sign out, these guys do this every day, today I'm along for the ride trying to get to understand a bit more outside of my little world that I see each and every day. I gather up my body armour, helmet and weapon and follow them out to the jetty at the rear of the palace. The two Boat Ops separate and take a boat each; I jumped in the nearest as we set off in the darkness from the Palace up the river. Despite the time it was still incredibly warm and humid but the breeze was refreshing as we sped across the water. Now, at this time of the morning the river was like a mill pond, during the day when the wind gets up it can be very choppy causing the boats to bang against the small waves. I was beginning to wonder how the boat ops could see anything as we were doing nearly 40mph and it was total darkness. Just then Kev, a Scottish Lance Corporal (I never knew his surname) produced a set of Night Vision Goggles and proceeded to look through them every few seconds to keep himself on course. I had never used NVG's before this. They show everything as though it was daylight except for the green tint in the viewfinder. He explained to me as he steered the boat with one hand, holding the monocular viewer with the other, the nature of today's patrol. We were going to pick up a patrol team from the '1 Kings Regiment' who were located in the old "Shatt Al Arab Hotel" on the banks of the river about thirty minutes away. Accompanying them would be a gaggle of press from many journals and newspapers each looking for their exclusive scoop and photo to take back to blighty. Both boats pulled into the jetty with Kev giving me the nod to jump out and secure the boat. Another guy called Ginge, (not the same guy I met in the house some time ago) manned the other boat. That's the thing about the army, you have to have a blindingly obvious nickname such as Taff if you're Welsh or Joc if you're Scottish or as we see here, Ginge if you are on the orange side of strawberry blonde. Both Kev and Ginge lived in the same house as me and although I have seen them every day for the last couple of months, I haven't a clue what the rest of their names are. I have known people in my unit in the UK for over twelve years, people whom I see all the time, people who I know exceptionally well and over

half of them don't know my first name... to them I am
simply 'Woody'.

The eight soldiers from the '1 Kings' climbed into the
other boat with Ginge, leaving Kev and me landed
with the press in ours. There were eight people in total
that clambered into our boat. Their kit was strewn
everywhere immediately. It seemed odd seeing people
dressed in brightly coloured civilian clothes, however
they had all been issued body armour. Under a small
torchlight, Kev briefed them on the safety aspects
involved whilst I helped kit them out with their life
jackets. On the boat were a mixture of people ranging
from the;
*"I've been in this war reporting industry for thirty years
and nothing shocks me... I've seen it all",*
To the guy with a holiday style camcorder who was
filming everything and smiling like a kid on Christmas
morning because he was off on a boat jolly up the
river.

There were two female journalists, a young Asian
woman who worked for the Manchester Evening News
and a woman in her mid thirties who worked for the
Daily Mail in London. The Asian girl was very friendly
and more than happy to chat, asking questions and
scribbling away formulating the answers into her
piece, the woman from the Daily Mail on the other
hand looked like she had just stepped off a catwalk
and hardly said a word, her hair was carefully
coiffered to within an inch of its life and enough
makeup to deflect any 7.62mm round from two
hundred metres, this woman obviously got out of bed
very early this morning to get herself ready for this

little boat trip. She sat very quietly letting everyone else ask the questions and she was there to grab the answers. Her time would come; I could see she was a far more experienced predator when it came to journalism. There was also a guy in his early forties who was a journalist for "4–4–2" magazine which is apparently a football magazine. I struggled to find the relevance of his trip relating it to football but still I answered his questions as best I could.

We set back down the river to retrace our route; it took about thirty minutes to get back to the Palace. En route I was asked to provide a bit of a talk about the area, the history of the sunken boats and the buildings as we passed. I gave the bits that I had picked up over the last couple of months and amazed myself at how much came spewing out. The journalists were scribbling away but the photographers were frustrated that they were redundant until the sun came up.

The CSB leaving the jetty at the Shatt Al Arab Hotel.

As we neared the Palace, it struck me that whatever I said they wrote it down. I fought the temptation to make up a story about Saddam standing naked on his balcony urinating into the river below, now that would have been a scoop for them to take back!!!

As the light began to lift, the joy ride had finished and it was time for the '1Kings' boys to do their job. They would operate from the other boat as our boat acted as voyeurs allowing the photographers to do their stuff.

The job of the team on the other boat was to patrol for smugglers approaching each and every boat they saw. They would pull up along side a chogie boat and instruct them to kill their engine and all stand up. Their boats are invariably long and thin sitting very low in the water, with a small outboard at the back providing the power. This is the type you would expect to see on a TV documentary in the jungle. Invariably they would stand up and immediately protest their innocence, as you do when you have eight soldiers pointing rifles at you at half five in the morning. One soldier would then board their boat and begin to search it for weapons, ammunition or anything suspicious. Once they were cleared they were allowed to go about their business. The river at this time of the morning is surprisingly busy, the majority are fishermen returning with their nets and a boat full of sardines, others are simply moving people from one side of the river to the other as the bridges are few and far between on this stretch of river.

_____

They stopped one boat full of women and children, carrying out the same drills as before. You couldn't help noticing the fear on their faces as they wondered what the hell was going on, not only with the weapons pointing at them from one boat, plus all these other people in brightly coloured clothes armed with cameras from the other. The mothers covered the heads of the children as their boat was searched. I felt very uneasy as this happened, as they were not ready or deserving of this vast intrusion into their lives, albeit I do understand that this has to take place to flush out the wrong doers who would otherwise be working against these people. We are here to make their lives better, we are also here to eliminate the minority that don't wish to lose the control over these people's lives with the grip that they have had for so long.

They were finally cleared and sent on their way, all were now smiling and waving back with great signs of relief, this was one of the boats carrying out a ferry service. I was told that that this boat had been stopped because it looked suspicious being a small boat loaded only with people yet it had such a large engine.

Kev said *"What are they doing so different that they can afford a large out board motor like that,?"* I could see his point.

We carried on doing more of the same stopping around seven or eight boats, the photographers now in their element as they clambered over each other trying to get 'The Shot' that would make their trip to Iraq worth while. I watched them as the searches were taking place and I could see the excitement in the eyes of one of them, one even licked his lips with anticipation as the motor on the camera whirred as he snapped away, stopping only to quickly change the lens and jockey for a better position on the boat. The guy with the holiday camcorder obviously wasn't aware of any photographer's etiquette such as; don't walk in front of the lens when the others are in the aim. What did he care, he was after his holiday video, he just moved up and down the boat grinning like a new born baby with wind, pointing his camera and filming everything like people do the first time they enter Disneyland's Main Street.

As the sun rose across the river on the horizon, the photographers were not to be disappointed. Using the PRR radios, they ordered the position of the other boat to be in the correct location to catch the light... adding that extra element to their shot. They then required some close up shots of a poor unsuspecting squaddie going about his daily business, and... as they were all on the other boat, the only people left were Kev who was operating the boat, and yours truly. Now although I looked the part, this was not my job, I really didn't have much idea other than what I had learnt this morning, adding insult to injury...I was only there to get a story just like them. Kev nodded to me as much to say, "You carry on sunshine... rather you than me". So, I got the job of posing like a geek for three photographers as they all ordered me into a variety of positions like a porn star. (Well I can but dream!!) One of them wanted me to straddle one of the large engines at the back of the boat as if sitting on a horse pointing my rifle at anything that dared to follow us, I sent him the *"you can f\*\*k right off"* look before I courteously explained that it would not be normal operating procedures.... as if I would know what normal operating procedures were on carrying out boat patrols, the bit that I did know was that you didn't do it looking like Roy Rodgers. Knowing my luck, that would be the photo that would have made it onto the front page of The Mail on Sunday and I would carry that as a legacy for the rest of my life...I can hear them now *"Oh look, there goes the twat who thought he was the Lone Ranger on his boat"*

Kev called time on their fun as they both had another operation following this, so we headed back along the river back to the Hotel to drop them off. It was now 0700hrs. As we pulled alongside the jetty they began to gather their kit as they all climbed out of the boat thanking us for our time, that is, all except for the guy with the holiday camcorder who proceeded up the jetty with kit hanging off him like Charles Hawtry in Carry on Camping, dropping most of it as he walked away.

*"F\*\*king Civvies"* Kev said shaking his head as they walked away,
*"Yeah, F\*\*king Civvies"* I said in agreement as they turned the boats round and set off down the river back to the Palace for some breakfast.

More to come...

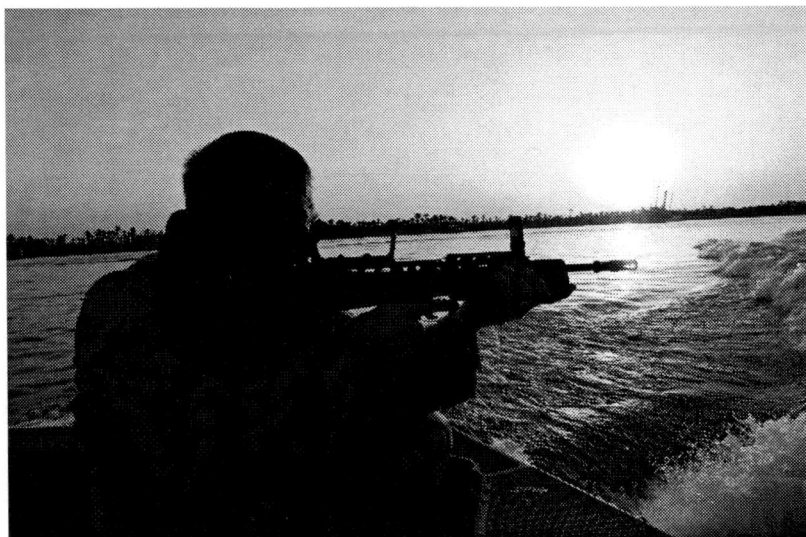

Here are two of the photos that were taken by the press with the sun coming up on the horizon. The engine they wanted me to sit on is behind me. (Photo Below)

## BUT HE'S GINGER!!!

21st September 2003

Counting down the days to the end of your tour is a regular occurrence here. Counting down to R&R (Rest and Recuperation) is the first milestone for most people. This consists of a flight back to the UK or wherever your home is. For a four-month tour you get seven days and for a six-month tour you get fourteen days. When you are removed from your normal life, the thought of returning to it can be a fantastic feeling. Some people count down to it mentally, others have a small calendar, ticking off the days in the way you would see a prisoner in a film. I saw Jools using an Excel spreadsheet that counted down to R&R and to the end of the tour. It not only calculated everything from days, hours, minutes and seconds etc. but also worked out how much he had earned and then drew pie charts of every aspect of calculation. This changed daily and became his first job every day in the Ops room, *"I'll just check my Chuff Chart"* he would announce proudly, and although some would ignore him others would glance with idle curiosity as their dates would be very similar. My date was given as 19th September for a seven-day break. I kept thinking "Only a few more days before my R&R", but it never seemed to get any closer. It amazed me how the MOD could slow down time prior to R&R and then speed it back up again once you were home.

The days before dragged painfully slow, but eventually it was the day. I was in the ops room all day, I felt like a kid on Christmas Eve wanting to go to bed early. During the day we got the news that we had to vacate our house and move into the new-tented camp that had been erected in the Palace Grounds. I couldn't believe it, not only had I got to pack for R&R but we had to move house as well, and all before I could go. As soon as I finished my shift in the Ops Room, I rushed back to the house to start moving my kit. There were plenty of people to help so it was all done and the house was vacated in a couple of hours. The new tents were tunnel shaped with hard floor matting inside, all joined together with a main body as the corridor and legs coming from that as the bedrooms, each sleeping eight people. The whole complex of tents had aircon but it didn't seem to be that effective. As I walked down the white tunnels for the first time it reminded me of the film ET when the scientists took over Elliott's house. Everything inside was white and brand new.

I set up my new bed space ready for my return and then finished packing my kit. I was going home. With my bags packed I signed my weapon and ammunition in and boarded the four tonne Bedford. On the back were eight other people who were ending their tour along with Jerome who was also going on R&R. There were two LandRover's giving an armed guard cover front and rear for our journey to the airport.

We left at 2300hrs and headed for the airport for a reporting time of midnight to catch a 0440hrs flight. As we all sat on the back of the flat surface of the Bedford, no one spoke a word, we all sat on the floor in the darkness, helmets and body armour on, my knees were up to my chest sitting completely silent as we clattered and banged across the potholes of Basra for the half an hour journey to the airport. I began thinking of all the things that I had missed the most from home:

They were:

- Kerry, my children and family,
- HJM's (Horizontal Jogging Manoeuvres)
- A nice glass of red wine
- Sitting on a white porcelain toilet at ambient temperature.
- Eating food without sweat dripping from my nose
- Rain
- Skateboarding

---

The list was endless but they were the top few.

After an eternity of waiting we finally boarded the plane only to find that we were flying via Cyprus first with a further three hour waiting time before completing the journey with a four and a half hour flight back to Brize Norton. I didn't sleep much on the journey, partly because there was no legroom and partly because of the excitement of getting home. I was so exited at the thought of seeing Kerry and the kids again I had to stop myself from smiling as my face was begging to ache.

On the approach to Brize Norton I was craning my neck to see through the clouds, I wanted to see the green hills of England. One cloud turned into another...and another, how deep are these clouds? Eventually we fought our way through and I got my sight, and... what a sight. You may have felt it yourself if you have been on a holiday of the package kind and spent two weeks somewhere hot and sunny, after months in the colourless and featureless surroundings of Iraq it appears greener than you could imagine. After we landed, I moved through to collect my luggage and then on through to arrivals where there were numerous family and friends of people waiting to greet their loved ones. A TV crew was there from BBC South Wales welcoming their boy's 'The Royal Monmouthshire Regiment' back home. I fought my way through the tears and gratuitous emotion that was flowing and proceeded to the desk to collect my hire car keys. My time would come.

The journey from Brize Norton to home takes around one hour fifty minutes, I quickly calculated that there was a sporting chance that I could make it back home in time to collect my children from school. Alex and Georgia attend a primary school in the village and Ashleigh attends a comprehensive school. Traffic permitting the Primary school was my first target. Kerry never told the children about my homecoming just in case it didn't come off. As far as they knew Daddy would not be home until just before Christmas.

After much bobbing and weaving my way through Friday afternoon traffic, I made it home at 1450hrs, twenty minutes early. As I drove up the High Street of the village, I couldn't stop drinking in the sights, the shops, the people, nothing had changed. As I turned into my road I started to smile, *"I'm home"* I thought to myself. I already had a lump in my throat and I hadn't got there yet.

I pulled the hire car onto my drive as I saw a shadow move inside. I was still in the same desert combats from my journey as I hadn't changed since leaving the palace yesterday, I dragged myself out of the car and after arching my aching back, stood still for a moment, looking across the front garden at Kerry as she stood on the front door step. I had forgotten how stunning she looks. Neither of us moved, we just stood there looking at each other. I moved around the car and walked down the path looking at everything, the path, the windows, the plants, it was all so familiar yet so surreal. Fighting the lump in my throat, I stopped and just managed to say, *"This is my home"* as we both burst into tears holding each other close. I could smell

the perfume on her, the same perfume she had posted
out months earlier. Finally... I am home.
It had been a very long time, a lot had happened, not
only to me but also to Kerry; we had a lot of catching
up to do.
There was hardly time for a quick chat before we had
to rush round to the school to meet Georgia and Alex.
Although it did cross my mind there was no time for
HJM's yet... well, in the two minutes we had spare it
probably would have been, but I fought that
temptation.

It felt weird having people staring at me as we walked
up the path towards the schoolyard. For months I had
worn this stuff and no one bats an eyelid, here... I was
out of place, people staring at us without any shame or
diplomacy. As we entered the playground I could see
more people pointing at us. Most people knew I was in
Iraq, few knew that I was coming home today.

The few minutes of waiting seemed to take an eternity;
eventually Georgia was the first to come out. Chatting
to her friend she walked slowly, then looking up she
finally saw me and when it registered in her mind she
ran across the playground screaming, *"It's my Daddy"*.
I immediately filled up trying to talk to her as I cried.
I crouched down holding Georgia when I saw Alex
emerge. Alex is nearly nine and is very cool conscious.
He saw me holding Georgia as he turned to his mate
and said, *"That's my Dad"*, before starting to cry as he
walked towards me wiping his eyes and staying cool.
By this time I was gone, crying like a baby and I didn't
give a shit what anyone thought. For the last few
months I had gone over it in my mind how I would

react when I got home, I would stay calm, cool and collected. That all went to rat shit the moment I saw my wife and kids.

Apparently there were a few of the parents in the playground who also got a bit tearful, but I was too preoccupied to think about anyone else. We gathered up the school bags and all walked home hand in hand.

Twenty minutes later it was the turn of our eldest daughter, meeting her off the school bus. At thirteen Ashleigh is also very cool conscious, but... also finds the embarrassment of having a parent in the same county, sometimes too much to bear if she is with her friends. So, if her Dad turns up at the Bus stop dressed like 'Stormin Norman', crying like a baby... it wouldn't do her street cred any good whatsoever.
As she alighted the bus she looked across and saw me immediately. She walked slowly towards me with her friends and simply said "Hi Dad" as her eyes filled; I knew she was pleased to see me.

We got back into the car and drove home. I was struggling to keep up with everyone telling me what had been happening, and everything that I had missed. Like the time Alex was playing with a cigarette lighter by the woods at the side of the house and nearly burned the house down. Two fire engines dealt with the burning trees and Kerry was left to deal with Pyro Boy.

After being home for about two hours, there was a knock at my front door, I answered it... and a Ginger Teenage youth pushed his way passed me and walked into my front room, I was left holding the front door handle and ready to strike when Kerry, rushed across to introduce us, *"This is Johnny, Ashleigh's boyfriend"*

As I picked my jaw up from the front room carpet, I realised how long I'd been away. Before I left, I had a lovely little twelve year old girl who called me Daddy and hated boys, Now I have a teenage daughter, who wears makeup, calls me *"Dad"* and is dating.

As they left the house to go... *'Out'*... I realised I had hit a milestone in my life, my daughter wanted to be with 'Him' more than me.

Arm in arm they walked up the path. I was just about to give him the *"lay one finger on her and I break your f\*\*ckin legs"* father's standard speech when Kerry stopped me and explained what a lovely lad he was and how much he had helped since I had been away.

Over the next few days we spent every second together, swimming, eating out, cinema, visiting family, friends at work, it was all going superb until the inevitable happened....................

More to come...

Before I tell you what happened next, I simply had to include this for your enjoyment. As you are aware my stream of long emails were now being circulated far and wide and read by a lot of people, and as a result, I have received many supportive emails back in return, This was a reply to my previous email:

———————————

| Subj | **An officer and a gentleman** |
|------|-------------------------------|
| Date | 07/10/2003 10:56:49 GMT Daylight Time |
| From: | Mike at Hepple |

*Hi Phil*

*Thanks for your last despatch from the front or rather the home front I should say. I can well imagine that there would be tears in the schoolyard, a really moving event.*
*But only Woody I thought, only Woody with his complete 'lack' of the theatrical would turn up at school dressed in combats to greet his kids. Yeh, you write it like it was all Richard Gere and officer and a gentleman, but I know you and I can imagine what it was really like.*

*I can just picture the scene 2.55pm and Woody has started his journey through the mean streets of the village having stopped only to apply camouflage boot polish to his face so as to blend in to the surroundings of his specially hired Ford Mondeo in the distinctive Sahara yellow. In the distance he can hear the hiss of the school buses air brakes as they arrive at the gates, not unlike the relentless hissing of those midnight desert storms thinks Phil...as his one man patrol winds its way through these once familiar streets. Phil's combat training enables him to maintain a low, almost invisible profile. He pauses only to slip* *through the various check points along the way ...the mini roundabout, the pedestrian crossing, look left look right,.. left,.. right,.. left,.. right, Phil shakes his head and pulls himself together - a Hercules transporter will take the soldier out of the desert, but it's not that easy to take the desert out of the man..."another time another place" he mutters as he turns his USRV ( unarmed sales rep vehicle ) into the high street. On either side he surveys shoppers, women with prams, the local bank clerk dashing out of the Nat West to grab a late lunch from the pork butcher...but not a chogie in sight.. Phil's training tells him that means nothing...every movement, every shadow, every open window, spells potential danger and risk ... but worse than that.. far far worse ,more significant, more serious, more terrifying to Phil than the danger posed by any grenade wielding ex republican guard chogie, is the risk that Phil now faces......The unthinkable prospect that no bugger is going to notice him.!.........no ticker tape?,........ no heroes welcome?.......  no f\*\*\*ing chance!.*

*Quick as a flash Phil's previous training kicks in.. not the 'ten a penny' square bashing, keep yourself alive type training that the army can give you, but real training the type only a fork lift truck field sales manager out on the road with 2 days to kill between appointments knows about. Quick as a flash he sounds his horn, a bent old woman standing waiting for the number 27 bus with her heavy shopping trolley turns in the direction of the beep (because she wants to know someone with a car ) Phil's over enthusiastic wave receives an instinctive response from the old lady and as Phil disappears and her wave subsides the* *old lady is left wondering "who the hell do I know who drives a Sahara yellow 1.6 Mondeo LX dressed in dusty combat gear, body armour and sand goggles - I want to know someone with a car but not that mad ba\*\*\*rd". But too late Phil is away down the road like Mr Toad horn beeping, lights flashing, spinning in his seat for those over the shoulder "nearly missed you there" waves, which he has made his own. As he rounds the corner the school is in sight, his children's school, his children who he hasn't seen for months, who's pictures he carries. He mounts the kerb and is out of the car in seconds, elbowing young mothers out of the way, keeping low, close to the walls, protecting his flank.... one or two mothers with pushchairs, chatting by the school door haven't noticed his arrival but that's soon remedied. "Attention CF troops...don't move!" as he drops to the floor into horizontal jogging manoeuvres position as if to crawl under some barbed wire that only his trained eyes have spotted...*

*And then it happens, he sees them and they see him, a defining moment, a moment they have all looked forward to for months the dad they haven't seen for months has crawled, scattering mothers and babies in all directions in full combat gear, body armour and sand goggles up the whole length of the playground to pick them up from school and is now lying there in sniper position to greet them....... well you can imagine the emotion in their little hearts and how they must have felt ......... "That's my Dad!" .... it's enough to make any kid cry.*

*Come on Woody come clean your readers need to know how it really was.*

*Anyway good to hear from you Pal. I guess the R & R is over now but the good thing is you're in the home straight. keep your head down your chin up and stay safe. Remember; keep the heroics for the school yard. Will email again soon.*

*Best Regards*

Mike and all your readers @ Hepple

So... back to the plot, as you may recall, it was all going well on R&R when..............the inevitable happened...

## HOMEWARD BOUND

30th September 2003

Having spent a fantastic week at home, I now found myself staring up at the lights in the roof of the building in Birmingham; I knew it was not going to be good news. I had the birds tweeting in a circle around my head, just like in the cartoons. I couldn't believe it, I had fallen doing something I had done a few thousand times before, I had a simple fall and I was in agony. As I climbed out of the six feet deep wooden bowl, I made my way to the reception office. Diane, the wife of the owner who was very keen to get me to a hospital so that they could deal with me in the appropriate manner, asked me some questions as to how it happened as I stood in the office at the entrance to Epic Skatepark. Playing it down I said I was OK and just needed a painkiller for my sprain, not willing to hand out pain relief she supplied me with a bag of frozen chips instead. I sat there pondering my future clutching the bag of chips against my wrist. I knew that if I went to hospital, they would immediately throw my arm in a plaster cast and I knew I wouldn't be able to return to Basra to complete my tour.

We are told prior to flying home on R&R, not to do anything stupid. Having done this sport pretty much none stop ever since I was nine years old, I have never considered skateboarding as stupid, in fact, over the last few years I have enjoyed it more than ever as my son Alex has taken it up and become better at eight years old than I ever was, both sharing and enjoying the father/son bonding experience expressed through our chosen sport, even though, at the ripe old age of thirty-eight, it's now not socially acceptable for a man of my years or calories to be flying up and down big ramps in a skate park. I always found this difficult to grasp when anyone asked me what my hobby was and I said skateboarding. If I said snowboarding or skiing, that would be OK, but mention skateboarding and people immediately picture kids making a noise on a B&Q car park late at night. All over the world were millions of people who were involved in the massive skateboarding invasion of the seventies. All these people didn't die... they had kids... and when their kids started growing up, they were then encouraged to take up the sport, carrying on themselves where they left off, only this time using better facilities than were ever available when they were kids, now only held back by a larger waistline and an inbuilt sense of fear that they didn't have when they were ten. But in their late thirties and early forties, they flock to some of the hallowed concrete havens from 'back in the day'. Dedicated websites such as: middle-age-shred.com help ageing skaters with a passion for skating far greater than their ability levels, reunite and continue to ride the concrete waves together until their limbs finally give up, or their wives finally confiscate their boards.

I still had a couple of days at home before I was due to fly back to Basra from Brize Norton, so, rightly or wrongly I chose to keep quiet about my wrist, that gave me time to see if it got any better on its own, in addition, allowing me to come up with a cover story that not only helped to save my credibility with my colleagues at the Palace in Basra, but also one that answered the question as to why I had not gone to the hospital sooner.

The fact was, I was on the last leg of my tour with as little as four to six weeks still to serve all depending on which flight I was due to come home on. Having done so much... and come so far, I couldn't face, not completing the tour. It's a bit like competing in a marathon when someone pulls you out in the last couple of miles because you have a blister and you still wish to continue. *"Let me limp the last mile...I'll be fine!"*
I know that if I had gone to hospital in the UK, the decision would have been made for me, they would throw a plaster cast on it and that would be the end; I wanted to take the chance that it was only sprained, getting better over a couple of days and at the very

worst, going to the Army Med centre at the Palace so they could give me some pain killers and put me on light duties for a few days until it felt better. Either way, I could complete my tour of duty for the last few weeks and not feel that I had let anyone down... least of all, myself.

The swelling had been and gone by the time it was time for me to leave, yet another set of tearful goodbyes were said to Kerry and the kids, as I set off for Brize in my hire car. I pulled away from the house as the children ran alongside the car waving and crying as I drove off. I turned on the radio in a bid to try to take my mind away from the emotion that was swirling round in my head. The holiday was over; it was now back to work.

The flight back to Basra was better this time than my first a few months back, because I knew exactly where I was going, what I would be doing and who with. There was nothing left to shock me anymore, it would simply be a case of keeping my head down and getting the last few weeks out of the way, before coming home in November in time for tea and medals with my family.

On the flight, I had time to come up with my cover story,

*"Just before leaving the house to fly back to Basra, I was playing football with my son for a last kick about on my front garden when I slipped on wet grass and pushed my fingers back. It wasn't very painful at the time and has since swollen up on the flight, I think I'll be OK..."*

---

"Perfect" I thought, I went over it so many times that I even believed it myself in the end.

Once back at the palace in Basra, I was in quite a bit of pain from carrying my bags, climbing up and down vehicles, putting on my helmet and body armour. I tried to pick up and hold my weapon in my right hand and I couldn't support its weight, my wrist just gave way with the pain, in short, all the very things that I would usually do as part of my job would now be impossible. The worst was yet to come. When I got to the med centre I tried to fill out a form with my basic personal details, name, rank, number. I failed, I couldn't hold the pen, this meant that I would be little or no use in the Ops room working radios, taking and relaying messages. This was my last hope. I began to feel like an outcast.

I was then told to report to the Field Hospital in Shaibah Logistic Base for an x-ray, it's about 25km away and, as usual for all transport moves, was a two-vehicle move with now a minimum of six people and top cover. I clambered into the back of the LandRover with the person providing top cover stood directly in front of me. I sat cradling my arm as we hit every bump on the journey. I said nothing, just gathered my thoughts wondering how long I would be in hospital before I would return to the palace to do my job.

I have never been in an army field hospital before and had visions of sitting around on sandbags waiting for a squaddie to come and wrap a first field dressing on my arm, give me a quick shot of morphine to kill the pain and write a letter 'M' on my forehead. I couldn't have been further from the truth. I entered what is essentially an 18' x 24' tent. The design of all army tents are such that they are all separate components, a standard frame, a wall and roof or end panels. This allows them to be joined or laced together to form larger buildings. In the various CF camps around Basra they are most commonly used for either accommodation or field kitchens and cook houses. In the hospital the main reception was at the end of the central corridor which was a mass of these tents extending for over two-hundred metres, all lined with white plastic material offering a variety of benefits including cleanliness, light reflecting properties and another layer to keep the searing outdoor heat at bay. The floor is smooth grey plastic matting that covered every bit of ground area on this massive hospital corridor.

Stemming off from the main corridor at right angles were more corridors of tents stretching around forty metres each, forming all the usual departments you would expect in a hospital, Reception, A&E, X-Ray, Surgery, Operating Theatre and a series of wards, furthermore, along the apex of each roof was a large tube feeding the air conditioning through the complex, keeping the temperature to a comfortable level. Ghurkha Royal Engineers built this place a few months earlier from scratch and bearing in mind where this place is, on a recently occupied Iraqi Airbase in the middle of the desert, it really was a fantastic achievement.

I went to the reception where I immediately swung into my cover story, it sounded great, if not a little unconventional. I was then moved for an x-ray. The NHS could do with learning a thing or two from the British Army; I was booked in, x-rayed, plastered and moved onto the ward all within half an hour, absolutely amazing, all the staff were very friendly and helpful, no sitting in a reception for hours in here, it was very refreshing and swift, if not a little 'Matter of fact'. It was then that I was delivered the bad news that would change everything for me. My wrist was broken, a clean break through the bone, and I was to be air evacuated out on the next flight, which was in four days time, until then, I would be on the ward. I was devastated; my tour was at an end.

The next four days dragged, I dreaded the daily visits by the military consultants, all of whom seemed to have about eight or so lower ranks accompanying them as a fundamental part of their training. They would walk along the ward one bed at a time as the consultant talked with each of the patients in turn, whilst his students would hang on his every word.

In here there were some horrific injuries, one guy had been shot in his arm by an American soldier who had a negligent discharge with his rifle when standing directly alongside him. He also proudly displayed the clipping taken from the 'Washington Times' telling of his story. The newspaper clipping was passed around the small group, each scanning it and then commenting to the soldier on his bravery. One woman was unconscious for two days from a road traffic accident involving an Iraqi vehicle, she had pipes coming out of her body all over the place with bandages everywhere, she was in a rough way. There was even an Iraqi man who had a badly injured leg and was under twenty-four-hour guard.

All these people had proper injuries, injuries that they could tell their grand kids with pride, all were lucky to survive, I just felt like a pratt... a fraud... my story was not only false but far more plausible than the way it really happened, it wasn't even caused in the same country. I would have loved to tell them that I was sliding down a rope from a Chinook when......... etc..etc..

I could feel my stomach knotting up as they approached my bed. Peering over his half cut spectacles the consultant, a Major in his early forties, picked up my file from the pocket on the end of my metal framed bed and read it, he paused as he read it again, he then looked up at his small audience and read out how it happened.

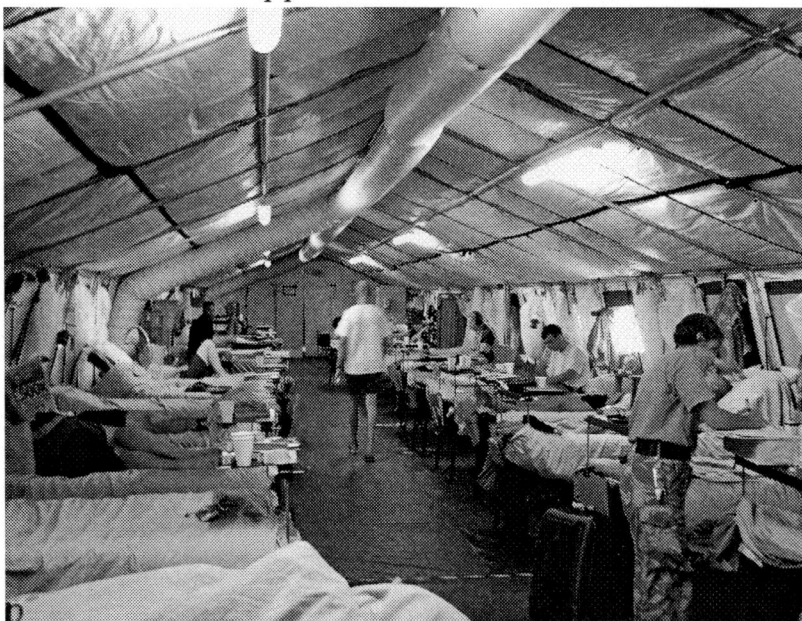

Sounding like there was a plum in his mouth he said *"Aahh this is an interesting one, this chappie was playing soccer on his drive with his son on R&R, he slipped and broke his wrist...My God man... what are you doing here?"* Immediately they all threw their heads back and laughed while looking at me as the centre of their amusement, at the time, all I could think of was *"Bastards, you've had your laugh... now f\*\*k off"* as I sat there with a false smile, reading my skateboard magazine. Every day he would come along the beds with a new crowd, and, when he got to me, he would take pride in telling his 'unusual' story to his new crowd of lower rank trainees, all of whom would throw their heads back laughing as before and as if they were listening to Billy Connolly live on stage. Those four days were mainly spent avoiding the "how did you break it" question, and taking a shower with a bright yellow surgical bin liner sellotaped over my arm.

Moving to the airport as an Aeromed case, you get escorted all the way, receiving a medical prior to take off and your own nurse to escort you during the flight, constantly checking you are OK, you even get a set of

Sat on the ward I read the obligatory 'Sidewalk' skateboarding magazine that Kerry would regularly post out to me to help keep me sane.

three seats to yourself on the plane, as all Aeromed cases have to be segregated from the rest on the flight in what they called a 'Cross Contamination Screen'. That suited me down to the ground as I got to lie down and get a bit of sleep with my own airhostess bringing me water when I needed it.

Once back in the UK I was escorted back to Chilwell in Nottingham to the same mobilisation centre I had passed through in early June. There I received another medical and a series of lectures including one on Post Traumatic Stress Disorder before being allowed back home.

I was experiencing very mixed feelings about coming home this time, I was looking forward to it, but I knew that this was the end of my journey. I chatted with the driver as we made our way back. When he got mobilised, his posting was in Chilwell, Nottingham, he went nowhere, I went to Iraq and Back. I spent a moment trying to figure out who was the lucky one, me for going or he for staying. As I was now safe I decided it was me, for going, but as I found out in August, it could have been a completely different ending.

He dropped me off on my drive as I dragged my bags down the path. Kerry ran up the pathway and threw her arms around me sobbing. She knew this time I was home for good.

It was a quiet moment for us both and a lot of relief for Kerry as she knew I would not be going back, also she tried to understand my disappointment in falling short of my end of tour date by a few weeks.

___

The next day I had to report to my local fracture clinic for the civilian doctors to now deal with me. I sat in the waiting room before being called through to see the consultant. He took my x-ray that was taken in Basra and slapped it under the light board, he paused then pondered for around twenty seconds, it was when he said *"Mmm, that's unusual"* that I thought he needed some help, so I mentioned to him that it was because the x-ray slide was back to front... as it clearly was. This was the first time that he looked at me like I was a piece of shit. Then he continued to ponder for a while longer, looking at the x-ray, I sat patiently watching him and couldn't help myself saying *"that's where it's broken look... there... along that white line"* I knew I should have kept quiet but I also knew I was right, because I had been looking at this x-ray for nearly a week with quite a few military medics and, a week later, I felt I was now an expert on my broken wrist. He once again gave me the 'piece of shit' look that he did so well, saying, *"I am a consultant surgeon specialising in hand and arm injuries, leave me to do my job"* I remember thinking, *"you couldn't be that f\*\*king good because you needed me to tell you that you had the x-ray the wrong way round"*
He then went away to make his notes directing me towards the plaster department.

As I left the hospital I pictured the surgeon in the pub that night laughing with his mates telling how he got his own back on a 'know it all' squaddie. I am now the proud owner of a full cast that not only goes from my knuckles to my armpit, but I also have my hand placed in such a way that I look like a camp mannequin in a shop window with my fingers sticking out backwards

so that I can't possibly hold a pint, and even if I could, I couldn't get it to my lips. To finish the whole look off, it's in fluorescent bright green.
Bastard!!!!

Everything now becomes a nightmare, getting dressed, getting undressed, eating, the new skill never tried before of wiping my arse left handed, the next six weeks will now drag, I have no doubt in that. I also find myself in unfamiliar territory, an area which I had not prepared myself for, but one that was inevitable.... the quick off the cuff comments that come from friends or colleagues that I am now finding myself struggling to deal with. The *What a great way to get out of it"* type of comment, the more I heard it the more angry I became. These people have no idea what it's like in Iraq and they think that it's great to be home irrespective of the consequences. My reason for going in the first place was to do the job I had been trained to do and not have to face myself every day for the rest of my life saying that I was a coward in not going. With these comments flying around it not only undermines every thing that I did but also tags me with a potential stigma of being the one who 'Got Out Of It' by breaking his wrist. I find myself trying to convince people of the truth, and of the fact that I wish I was still out there finishing the last five weeks of my tour. As the weeks go by I become very angry inside and sick of talking about Iraq, everyone wants to know how it was, almost as if I had just returned from Disneyland and was summing up the highlights of riding on Space Mountain. Time and time again I realised that people only wanted the headlines of interest and not the colour supplements of detail, a quick answer that was enough to fill around ten seconds and no more, any longer and I began to watch their eyes glaze over with boredom. It took me a long time to get to the quick *"hot, boring and scary all rolled into one"* answer polished off but if you ask me now, that's as much as you get. I have even had a few people ask the ridiculous question,

*"Did you enjoy it...? Was it fun?".*

The first time someone asked me this I just started shaking my head in total disbelief at what he had said, I couldn't believe it, where the f**k does he think I've been. I took a deep breath and tried to make light of it by saying;

*"I've done both fun and enjoyment in the past, I remember what they felt like......, it was laughter and happiness,...... it was sitting on a beach, ...... it was playing with my kids in the garden,...... it was having a great meal,...... this didn't fall into any of those categories, so I guess the answer is......No"*
He looked back at me feeling as though he had been verbally beaten up. I'm not sure that I knew whether I was being humorous or on the close edge of sarcastic, I started by going for funny but ended up with a slight hint of angry. He wished he hadn't asked, and to be fair I wish I hadn't answered.

I'd been warned about the mood swings and feeling angry, even guilty, knowing that a lot of my pals were still out there. I thought to myself, to have mood swings like that must be a load of crap, people that have mood swings just need to snap out of it, maybe get a bit more sleep and decent shag first thing in the morning, that should sort them out and set them up for the day. It's not something that I have suffered with in the past so why should I be any different now. The fact was... Kerry and the kids found me very difficult to live with for a while, I began snapping at the slightest thing, even shouting at the kids for almost no reason, the very kids that I dreamed about being with... only six weeks ago. We had all gone through so much, from being apart for so long to looking forward to coming home, the elation of being back together and then finally the normality of the new routine, the living together once more, being in each others way, the *'I just want to sit and do nothing'* feeling when in fact Kerry wants me to help tidy up, do some house work, tidy the garden, cut the grass. All the usual man duties that lie around any family home. A lot of change has to take place.

I have an appointment set for next week to return to the mobilisation centre in Nottingham where I receive my military medical, as I am technically still on tour and receiving full military pay, therefore they need to make sure that I am following every step that is required when you're on a sick note from the MOD. Every week I visit my local hospital to get my medical assessment, x-ray and consultation and then report it back to the MOD doctor the next day. Finally I get the date that the cast will come off, so I arrange with the Mobilisation centre a day for De-Mobilisation. I can now plan for the belated summer holiday that the family should have had in July but was cancelled at three weeks notice. Kerry and I went to the travel agents and booked a holiday for my family in just four weeks time, just two weeks after the cast comes off and I get demobbed.

With the cast now off and my arm as thin as a super models, I gather up all my kit and return to Nottingham one last time for the demob process which is the exact reverse of what I originally went through back in June. The only difference being that I would now be on my own. As I drove through the main gates I couldn't help but look across at the exact same place that I sat a few months earlier. It was late in the evening of the first night; I sat with some people I didn't know then, Ossie, Elvis and Billy, all joking about what we could be doing in a few weeks. I remember thinking to myself as I sat on the wall that evening, *"I'm not sure that I'll be going to Iraq, this time tomorrow I could be back home"*.

I parked my car in the main car park and walked across the square with nothing more than the paperwork that had become my life, ID cards, dog tags, theatre pay and allowance card and medical documents, all were safely parcelled in a clear plastic sleeve... now well worn from the last few months. I left my kit in my car knowing that I could fetch it later. It was the same faces that I met in June during the mobilisation process, only this time it was quiet as I was on my own and being demobilised, there was no rapid fire rhetoric demanding that I do this, this, this and this and sit over there. The building now had a certain quietness about it, all was calm. Now I am getting briefed on returning as a civilian and how it may affect me, understanding the lines of communication should I need to contact anyone for help re-adjusting. I took my clip board and moved around the cells getting ticks in all the boxes once again, dental, medical, returning kit and finally the finance desk. During the financial cell I was given a certificate thanking me for my commitment and contribution to the regular army. The final date was set for my last day as a regular soldier and final payment date set following my few weeks of post tour leave. Soon I will officially be a civvy again.

My final task was to collect my MFO box that I had filled before leaving. The box that I had dumped all the surplus kit that I would not need, was sat waiting for me once more. I tried to remember what I left behind but struggled to recall its contents. I gave the issuing corporal my name, rank and number as he escorted me around a warehouse full of cardboard boxes looking for the aisle and location of my box. There it was... I pulled it out and signed my name. Using my car keys I cut the brown tape to gain entry. As I cut open the large flaps of the box I saw my message and I gave a huge smile as I read it once more,
*'Welcome home you slender suntanned handsome bastard'*

*"Ah well"*, I thought to my self, *"one out of three isn't bad... I've got a suntan!"*

# RETURNING TO NORMALITY

## 5th January 2004

In the last five weeks we have had both our summer holiday and our Christmas holidays and all that I am left with now is a very slender bank account and a very swollen waistline. I find myself again in a nerve-wracking position, returning to work.... A civvy, seven months after saying goodbye to my work mates, organising my wedding, getting married, saying goodbye to my family and packing my bags and setting off to Iraq. Now for the first time it all seems to have gone quickly.

The alarm went off at 6.30am, I got up and took a shower, had a shave and then pulled out a shirt from the wardrobe, in went the cufflinks, on with the tie, on went the suit and finally the shoes. I stood looking at myself for a while in the mirror in the bedroom. I hardly recognised this person in front of me. The shirt collar cutting into my neck, today, I start work again.

So here I am at the end of my long journey, preparing myself to return to my original world of managing a sales team selling forklift trucks.

I left the house and got into my car, suit jacket hung up in the back, mobile phone in its cradle, laptop in the boot and the radio on. I left the village and pulled onto the motorway rejoining the rat race once more. It's now that I remembered one of the things I had missed; talking to my best mate, Phil, each and every morning as we drive to work. We would be putting the world right and sharing our problems. We would always chat about nothing in particular and moan about everything.

Today I had a smile on my face; here I sit on the M6 motorway, parked up in the middle lane going nowhere, handbrake on in completely stationary traffic, with the tones of Terry Wogan wafting from the speakers. I decide to move my steering wheel up an inch... and then back again... only because I can. I look down at the cuff links, the shiny shoes, adjust my tie in the rear view mirror and think how far this is from what I had considered to be the norm with sand and sweat. I wonder how many other people sitting in this traffic jam would have anything interesting to say about what they had done different in the last few months... other than face the daily grind to work worrying about how they are going to have enough time to fit in both the pottery class and visit the mother-in-law on Thursday evening. My point is this, whatever you do in life, no matter how different, difficult or challenging, it is what makes you who you are... it's what gives you the after dinner stories that you will dine out on from here to eternity. I know all tours to the same place are different, my tour was no more, or less challenging than anyone else who went out there, I know there were people who had it much worse, I know that there are those that did not come home. Each person will have his or her own experiences and every single one will be different. I am certainly no one special, I did not do anything out of the ordinary, if anything, I shit myself with fear a little too often for my liking, not with fear for myself but for what my family would face should anything happen to me. I am just a bloke who did what was asked of him, and chose to throw something down on paper pointing out the bits that I, as a recent civilian, found unusual or interesting.

Eight months earlier I would have been pulling my hair out sat in a traffic jam like this, but not today, I am now totally relaxed, I am comfortable, not too hot... not too cold... the radio is on... I can phone who I want, when I want and no one is shooting at me, if I want a drink I can pull off the motorway and buy a drink. I also know that whatever happens at work today, no matter how horrendous the issue, I will still be sat down this evening at home eating my dinner with my wife and children, laughing about what we all did today, tell me it doesn't get any better than that.

---

I eventually pulled into the car park and positioned the car in a corner out of the way. I wasn't sure exactly what kind of reception I would receive, and if I had my choice the day would be like any other day, with a quick *"good morning, are you well?"*
*"Yes thanks... and you?"*
*"Fine thanks, see you later!"*

I just wanted to get back to work and start flying the star ship enterprise from my email cockpit once more. I couldn't wait to hear from my Sales Team, to see how well they did at the end of the financial year, have there been any changes in the company...what's the latest on the staff gossip, has anyone left, who's new to the team. All the type of stuff you like to catch up on, having been away for two weeks on holiday, seven months away must give me a feast of gossip, and the best bit of all, I call no one SIR!

I made my way to the reception. It was as if I hadn't been away, the same people doing the same things. I stood at the front desk and signed in as usual, it was a fantastic feeling, everyone that I met wanted to shake my hand and welcome me back. As I walked through the building I found myself saying the same things, over and over again. Trying to find the balance between answering their questions without sounding like Uncle Albert from 'Only Fools and Horses'.
The questions flowed thick and fast from everyone,

*"So what was it like then"* or *"How many people did you shoot"*. It was really was great to be back at work once more in the surroundings that were so familiar to me.

---

A part time soldier and their immediate family make huge sacrifices and adjustments in their daily lives to accommodate the change that is necessary when getting mobilised.
The only people who will truly understand what others like us have been through are those that have served with the armed forces in their time and have experienced the Heat, Fear and Boredom of conflict. Only they truly know what it's like to be away from home for long periods of time and not know if today is the last day you will be alive.

I was still struggling with the few people in the office that didn't know what to say and resorted to taking the piss.

*"Oh you're back from your holiday playing soldiers then, have you come back to do some real work?"* said one guy

*"You be careful not to break a nail when you're typing"* I said biting through my lip with instant anger and rage. I have learned now not to react to other people's ignorance and just let it wash over me. To them, high pressure and stress is having a few things to do after attending a meeting.

In Iraq currently (January 2004) there are over 14,000 British troops made up of Regular, Reservists and TA soldiers. Every single one gets my utmost respect. Whether or not you believe the government in its weapons of mass destruction argument for going to war in the first place, to me, is irrelevant, the fact is that every day our British Troops are delivering a better life for the people of Southern Iraq in extremely difficult conditions, and, one day in the future the Iraqi people will understand what life can be like without a dictator and to live in a democracy where freedom of speech is the norm. I was extremely proud to play a small part in that.

Would I go again? I think there are enough people in the TA to all play an active part in this, I also believe that if you wear the uniform and take the money then you must do the job asked of you when the time comes.

Was it an experience I will remember? Oh Yes... it helps you take a reality check on things that are important in life.

I have been asked by many to explain my reasons for writing a book, with some commenting that I was cashing in on the war and saying that it's morally wrong. In fact this is to be the opposite with it costing me money to see my work in print. I have no desire to become the next Booker prizewinner.
My reason for writing the book was very simple. I have a vision that one day in the future; my children can read about what Dad did when he went away to that place they heard about on the news each and every day. They would be able to give this book to their children and say *"that's what your Granddad did in 2003"*. To leave your mark in anything you do has to be a good thing for your family.
Finally I would like to point out that the person who deserves the medal from this should be my wife Kerry, for being on her own with the children and surviving.

On the few occasions that I have looked after Ashleigh, Alex and Georgia for anything more than a few days, has always completely worn me out with the house being reduced to a wreck within a matter of a few hours. I am usually left looking out of the window longing for Kerry's car to pull onto the drive and take over the controls once more.

On many occasions, the loved ones left at home have it just as bad as the people serving away from home. When you are out there, you know when to worry because you are in danger, you know when not to worry because you are in a safe area. The family at home will worry all the time and not be able to differentiate. To them, your homecoming is the only time they will stop worrying.

I hope you have had as much enjoyment from reading about my experiences as I have had from writing them.

There is, ....................no more to come!!!!

Well.... That is until the next letter hits the mat.

During one of our many days out, now we are together once more.

ISBN 1-41204543-6